A New Song: Celibate Women in the First Three Christian Centuries

D0082611

A New Song: Celibate Women in the First Three Christian Centuries

Jo Ann McNamara

A New Song: Celibate Women in the First Three Christian Centuries was originally published in 1983 by The Haworth Press, Inc. It has also been published as *Women & History*, Numbers 6 and 7, Summer/Fall 1983.

Harrington Park Press
New York • Binghamton

ISBN 0-918393-17-5

Published by

Harrington Park Press, Inc.
28 East 22 Street
New York, New York 10010

Harrington Park Press, Inc., is a subsidiary of The Haworth Press, Inc., 28 East 22 Street, New York, New York 10010.

A New Song: Celibate Women in the First Three Christian Centuries was originally published in 1983 by The Haworth Press, Inc., under the same title. It has also been published as *Women & History,* Numbers 6 and 7, Summer/Fall 1983.

Library of Congress Cataloging in Publication Data

McNamara, Jo Ann, 1931–
    A new song.

    Reprint. Originally published: New York : Haworth Press, 1983.
    "Has also been published as Women & history, numbers 6 and 7, summer/fall 1983"—T.p. verso.
    Bibliography: p.
    Includes index.
    1. Celibacy—Christianity—History. 2. Asceticism—History—Early Church, ca. 30-600. 3. Feminism—Religious aspects—Christianity—History. I. Title.
BR195.W6M35   1985   306.7'32'09015   85-8505
ISBN 0-918393-17-5 (pbk.)

About the Author

Jo Ann McNamara is Professor of History at Hunter College of the City University of New York and a founding member of the Institute for Research in History. She is the author of *Gilles Aycelin: A Servant of Two Masters* and translator of Pierre Riché's *Daily Life in the World of Charlemagne*. With Barbara J. Harris, she has edited *Women and the Social Structure: Papers from the Fifth Berkshire Conference on the History of Women.*

CONTENTS

Acknowledgements

This is a feminist work and, as such, it owes much to the ideas developed collectively in feminist circles. I cannot sufficiently acknowledge my debt to the members of the Family History group of the Institute for Research in History, the Faculty Development Seminar of Hunter College, the Women and Society Seminar of Columbia University and the Berkshire Conference on the History of Women. The present book was, in fact, conceived directly through this network. I want specially to thank Marjorie Lightman of the Institute for Research in History for urging me to make a contribution to the *Women and History* series and Eleanor Riemer, the series editor, for her high editorial standards which have constantly challenged me to give of my best.

Many friends helped me by discussing various aspects of this book with me. A few had the kindness to read it through and offer critical suggestions for the final revision. These were Blanche Cook, Marilyn French, John Halborg, Barbara Harris, John Nichols, Sarah Pomeroy, Thomas Renna, Nancy Siraisi, Steve Weinberger and Barbara Welter. I have tried to answer their criticisms in the final draft, but my own mistakes and my own stubborn convictions remain impervious to their efforts. As always, the hero of the effort is my son, Edmund Clingan, whose support and unflagging assistance have always lain at the foundation of my life.

To Edmund Clingan

For all our adventures together

Introduction

It is traditional to start the history of Christian asceticism with the flight of Saint Antony to the desert followed by the organization of monasteries in Egypt and Syria and a discussion of the great theoretical system constructed by Jerome, Ambrose, Augustine, and the other promoters of virginity from the fourth and fifth centuries. In fact, it was my original intention to do very much the same thing in writing the history of ascetic women. At the beginning of my work, however, I was caught by an event which occurs in the first chapter of Athanasius' work on the life of Antony. Before the so-called "father of monks" could answer his vocation, he was obliged to make provision for the care of his orphaned sister. He solved the problem by placing her in a house of consecrated women.[1] Clearly the history of the ascetic woman did not begin with Antony's flight. It has a prehistory out of which the present book has grown.

It may be difficult for the modern reader to realize that the virginal life was only fully sanctioned by orthodox writers after women had made it a practical reality. The enthusiasm of the patristic writers of the fourth and fifth centuries set the seal of approval on their way of life, but before they found admirers, the virgins had withstood many critical attacks. The celibate life was a life that certain women chose to live. It was not foisted upon them by men and, to some extent, the attitudes of Christian Fathers should be viewed as reactions to the activities of women, not their initiators. That is the viewpoint that has governed me in writing this monograph. The authors of our sources were sometimes misogynists and sometimes they were champions of the rights of women. More often, their attitude toward women was secondary to the purposes for which they wrote. Generally, I have not addressed the question of their motives because my purpose has been to try and discover the women of the celibate communities themselves, not to psychoanalyze their male co-religionists. This is a study of the women who carved out a new niche for themselves in the social structure; who came to sing a new song before the Lord.

These were women who disturbed the social order. In an age

when women's role was viewed primarily as procreative, and the state itself reinforced their familial and domestic functions, they chose not to engage in any sexual activity at all and to live independent of men. These were chaste widows and virgins who came to see in Christianity the opportunity to make a new place for themselves in the public sphere, one which would validate their condition and even, eventually, bring them praise for their way of life.[2] These women came to identify celibacy (which simply means "unmarried") with the assexual life, and to define virginity as a voluntary profession rather than a transitional phase in the life of a young girl.

The first generation of Christians knew prophets and visionaries who denounced the material world and sexuality and connected salvation with rejection of the flesh and all its works. Among male gnostic philosophers and Jewish ascetics, this attitude contained no small amount of mysogyny; they associated women with procreation, which they believed was the source of all evil. The same attitudes were found in the writings of the Fathers of the church, though there they were limited by the Christian commitment to the goodness of God's creative achievement. It is probable that among ascetic women this attitude was reversed, as it often was in the apocryphal gospels whose anonymous authorship may cloak a female statement.[3] There, men, not women, appear as the agents of the hated lusts of the flesh.

To write about these women is no simple task. We know their achievement: the celibate community. What we can learn of its accomplishment, however, must be gleaned primarily from indirect and often critical sources. It is very like trying to reconstruct a conversation from only one side. We hear answers but not the questions. We hear rebuttals but not the assertions. We hear sermons but we do not know who was listening. Nevertheless, I have attempted to write a book from the point of view of the unheard participant in this dialogue. I am painfully aware that the project is dangerous and the ground shifting and unsteady under my feet. As far as possible, I have tried to avoid lengthy discussions of motive and psychology and build my case on the socially observable activities noted by their friends and critics. Even under this restriction, the outcome of their struggle was immeasurably important to all women who have followed them into the public sphere.

These women conceived and carried out a revolution of vast proportions. They forced the social structure of antiquity to incorporate the celibate woman in a secure and even superior stratum. Some of the men who commented on the process were hostile and fearful of the new order they saw developing in their midst. Others were friendly, consecrated to the new ideal themselves. But, on both sides, they could not see their sisters except as "the other," who represented archetypal temptations or supreme purity. Thus they tended to conclude that she was an "other" who might be best advised to live silent and veiled so as not to disturb or provoke her brothers. The barriers between women and men had been strong in the ancient world, fortified by uncompromising gender roles, legal restraints, and religious taboos. In our period, emancipated women who took advantage of the spreading anomie of the Empire were treated by satirists with savage contempt. For the most part, they had no language and no concepts to formulate an answer or to define themselves beyond the biological conveniences of men. They remained simply "unmanly" possessors of all those negative personality traits unsuited to the virile identity.[4] Thus, when the single woman whose own voice has broken through to us speaks, she tells us that when she had put aside her conjugal ties, said farewell to her father and mother and given up her baby to them before her impending martyrdom, she became a man.[5]

Jesus' message held an inherent hatred of social barriers, an anarchistic impulse to turn the world upside down. The idea of a world with no marriage or giving in marriage, a society of neither male nor female, attracted many women. The unstructured new religion that spread through the Empire offered, among its other attractions, a strong individualistic message which some women used to break the barriers of "otherness" and create a positive new identity grounded in celibacy, and transcending the gender system.

That ancient gender system rested on the belief that the female body was inferior to the male and periodically polluted. It was almost axiomatic that women's minds were feeble and their morals hopelessly corrupt. The public sphere that men inhabited was systematically sealed and secured against the contaminating influence of women. In general, men were fairly well protected from any chance that women might find the means of refuting their prejudices. But in the individualistic climate of imperial Rome, this happy segregation between men and those who were not men was being eroded rapidly. In fact, in the first generation, many Christians appear to have welcomed this structural dissolution as a sign of the coming Kingdom.[6]

But, as time passed, many more men became frightened and

would have refilled Pandora's box if they could. This is the story of the ensuing struggle between women who wanted to move into a larger sphere and their male co-religionists who all too often reacted with attempts to segregate them, keep them out of the church, and protect themselves against the threatened breakthrough. However, these same men were anxious to convert women and find a place for them under the authority of the emerging male clerical hierarchy. In reading the prescriptive literature of early Christianity, we too readily imagine that the women to whom it was addressed were docile subjects of their clerical guides. It required perseverance and courage in no mean measure to embrace and maintain the religion during the centuries with which this study is concerned. Most of our subjects were not born Christians. They chose the faith and its teachings.

What did they find in Christianity and in the celibate life which they embraced? During the writing of this monograph, many of my friends have asked me why I think that these women were prepared to suppress their own sexuality, to deny themselves the physical and emotional satisfactions of marriage and motherhood. In the absence of any direct testimony from these women I have tried to avoid too ready an answer. Here, in the introduction, however, I have determined to advance a few conjectures. A fear and hatred of men is the possibility most ready to hand.* Gnostic literature, the apocryphal gospels, and the tracts in praise of virginity that come from later ages all advance the humiliation of sexual intercourse and the pain of childbearing as reasons to turn away from the procreative life. From there, it is simple enough to argue that there is immense attraction in the choice of Mary of Bethany. Many women must have been eager to leave the burden of housekeeping in favor of a life of spiritual devotion and active involvement in the affairs of the infant church.

Let me now go one step farther. The most congenial marriage is in many respects emotionally limiting and so is even the most fulfilling maternal experience. The conditions of women's lives tended to confine them to their homes and, consequently, severely limit the range of relationships open to them. There is a fair amount of evidence that women who turned to celibacy broke through those

---

*I was prevented by my gentle editor from the use of the word "misanthropy," which dictionaries generally define as "hatred or distrust of all people." There is, therefore, no corresponding term for "misogyny," a state of the language that seems to make a strong statement of its own.

limitations and achieved relationships with men that were of a completely different order. The romance of Paul and Thecla centers on a celibate pair, sometimes travelling together but more often living separately, who shared a profound spiritual union which grew out of their mutual devotion to a higher purpose. Only critics describe the lives of the *subintroductae,* who set up chaste households with male clergymen, but they must themselves have found satisfactions in that companionship that made them willing to risk the resulting scandal and persecution. Even critics are silent regarding the further possibility that celibate women may have been entranced by their discovery of one another. In their communities, their religious activities, their shared households, these women, perhaps, discovered a sisterhood that offered them emotional rewards that few women before them ever had a chance to know.

What is clear is that women found the celibate life one that was worth struggling for. That for some women, it was the price of their adherence to Christianity. This study represents but a first chapter in the long history of the struggle of Christian women to find a spiritual fulfillment in the church of their faith. The creation of a community of consecrated women, taking pride of place in the celestial hierarchy, represents the first fruit of that contest. The virginal ideal was not imposed on women by men fearful of their own sexuality. It was a revolt against an earlier set of male definitions, a rejection by some women of the sexual roles they had played so long. No early Christian father recommended virginity to women until they had already claimed it as a new role for themselves in Christian society.

FIGURE 1. Christ healing the woman with an issue of blood. Rome, Catacomb of SS Pietro e Marcellino. From Grabar, André, *Early Christian Art* (New York: Odyssey Press, 1968), plate 51.

Chapter One: The Better Part

Jesus was often criticized for the dubious company he kept.[1] He answered his critics that, when the new kingdom came, the tax collectors and harlots who followed him would take precedence over the righteous who were unbelieving and ungenerous.[2] He preached that old boundaries would be broken and old hierarchies turned upside down. He promised his followers that the poor widow and the repentant harlot, with the humble tax collector and the charitable Samaritan, would be first in the Kingdom of Heaven. These were the believers who would become the preachers of the Gospel and the founders of a new religion.

The Women From Galilee

The first women to embrace the message were Jewish, most of whom came from Galilee, an area whose very name betrayed the continual incursions of Gentiles among its inhabitants (Galil-ha-Goyim). The ruling house of Herod, which still maintained its independence from Roman rule despite the occupation of neighboring Judaea, welcomed Hellenized colonists to the major cities of Galilee, Bethsaida, Capernaum, and Magdala. Thus Jesus and most of his original followers came from that part of the ancient kingdom of Israel most constantly affected by outside influences with their attendant psychological and social disturbances.[3]

The scanty sources available to us from this period throw little light on the society and psychology of the Galileans. Since Galilee was not then under Roman rule, they may have been indifferent to the political agitation of the anti-Roman Zealots in Jerusalem. Furthermore, the strict regulations and demands of the temple priesthood in Jerusalem may have irritated the people of this more cosmopolitan land. The Gospel of John suggests a strong sense of alienation and even hostility between Judaeans and Galileans.[4]

Jesus preached in synagogues and in fields to large crowds, often drawn from as far as Syria and the cities of the Phoenician coast. Women and children were present among those who, on one occa-

sion, camped in the open for three days, listening to him until their
food gave out and his helpers had to gather a paltry gleaning of
loaves and fishes to feed them.[5] These crowds did not collect by accident; they were drawn together by the advance preaching of Jesus'
followers who fanned out in every direction with the news. Among
these, of course, were the twelve apostles, known by name, whom
Jesus appointed for the task. Seventy other persons, whose names
and genders are not known, were similarly commissioned to preach.[6]
Mindful of the vastness of the task, Jesus prayed for yet more laborers to take up the burden.[7] Once, we know, he chose a woman, a
Samaritan, whom he sent back into a nearby city. She returned with
a crowd whom he instructed for two days.[8]

In theory, there should have been no unmarried women among
the followers of Jesus.[9] Jewish females were expected to marry at
puberty. Although ancient tradition reserved a young girl's right to
refuse a marriage arranged by her parents before she matured, it did
not give her the right to reject marriage itself, which was prescribed
for all Jews. The practice of polygyny was still very much in force.
Its most striking expression was the levirate marriage, which obliged a man to take the wives of his dead brother in marriage and
beget children with them in his brother's name.[10]

In this period, however, most Jewish men probably found one
wife a sufficient burden on their financial resources and shunned the
responsibilities of additional marriages, if possible. Even the levirate could be avoided through the public ritual of repudiation if the
widow had been able to find another husband.[11] Indeed, heavier
economic burdens on men in this urbanizing society were sometimes
balanced by the increased economic independence of women, both
of which tended to discourage polygyny.[12] Nevertheless, many first-
century Jews defended their traditional polygynous practices very
strongly against Roman pressures for universal monogamy.[13]

Every couple was expected to procreate. Even a man who wished
to live without sexual relations was first required to generate two
children. After that, he was supposed to divorce his wife if he intended to deprive her of her right to sexual satisfaction. Otherwise,
the whole question of divorce remained unsettled at the time. Traditional opinion held that a man should not divorce the wife of his
youth and, indeed, there was little reason why a man should have
done so, since he could add a younger wife to his household if he
wished.[14] The Rabbi Hillel, however, defended a man's right to
divorce his wife at his pleasure. His opponent, Shammai (whose

party apparently influenced Jesus), disapproved of divorce except for adultery, a crime which only a woman could commit.[15] According to the Gospel of Matthew, Joseph came very close to putting Mary away because of her untimely pregnancy.[16]

Needless to say, women were not expected to initiate any divorce actions. In Jesus' time, the nature of woman's right to refuse a marriage was hotly debated, and the opposing views eventually were recorded in the Talmudic code of the second and third centuries. Hillel wished to expand a girl's right of refusal to include a marriage already consummated, if it had been contracted by her parents while she was under age. He even approved of the right to refuse the levirate obligation, where it might be imposed on an older widow whose first marriage had been premature. In short, Hillel would have deprived parents of virtually all their power to force a young girl into an unwanted marriage. Shammai, on the other hand, felt that consummation invalidated the right of refusal.[17]

However, in Jesus' time, the rabbis represented only a sect within a larger Judaism. They were arguing within a social context where parental power was still very much alive and was reinforced by the laws of the state. In general, the subjection of women to men— either fathers, brothers or husbands—was a virtually unquestioned fact of life in the first century. Paul (or his interpolator) would cite that subjection as the unavoidable barrier to female leadership in Christian communities.[18] His contemporary, Philo of Alexandria, was a fierce defender of the continuing subjection of women in Judaism,[19] and the strengthening of the authority of fathers over their children of both sexes.[20]

The subjection of women within marriage took several shapes. Their physical functions related to menstruation and childbearing were regarded as unclean, and their movements and activities were restricted to avoid contaminating men. Economic restrictions reinforced the psychological and social effects of purification requirements. Though women were legally supposed to enjoy economic protection through paternal endowments and marital settlements, they rarely had the free disposition of these revenues. They had good reason, therefore, to fear the economic and social repercussions of their husbands' displeasure. Men could divorce their wives at will, even though some rabbis advised against it.

Moreover, though law and its attendant customs still bound women to the family matrix, the accidents of real life often left them unprotected and isolated outside their prescribed and accustomed spheres. As we shall shortly see, many of the women around Jesus appear to have occupied such marginal positions: some were widows; others seem to have had no husbands and may have been the victims of capricious divorce; some of them, through penury or willfulness, had pursued adventurous sexual lives; others were reduced to begging. They formed a motley company who responded to Jesus' teaching and enlisted among his most faithful followers.

The women of Galilee may also have felt somewhat alienated from the centralized Temple priesthood in the old capitol of David. The histories of Jesus and his predecessor, John the Baptist, suggest that Galilee may have been more inclined to a prophetic religion than to the temple-centered worship of Judaea. But Galileans certainly worshipped at the Temple on various special occasions, as the New Testament illustrates.

Though worship in the Temple involved women as well as men, they were, of course, not included in the priesthood or given sacerdotal roles. At certain points in their lives, women went to the Temple for purification and for the celebration of various communal and family feasts. The Gospel of Luke depicts Mary praying in the Temple when the angel announced that she would be the mother of Jesus.[21] Anna, the prophetess, was said to have spent virtually all her time there.[22] The Temple, therefore, seems to have been available to women as a place of private prayer, within certain limitations. Philo of Alexandria argued that women should visit the Temple only when the men had gone, in order to avoid giving offense by their presence.[23] Harsh as his attitude is, it suggests that women were not strictly segregated or confined to an invisible area of the precinct.

This view conforms with the general loosening of strictures against women that we find elsewhere in the Hellenistic and Roman societies in this period. Indeed, the inclusion of the books of Esther and Judith in the last formative period of the Jewish Bible suggests a real interest among religious Jews of the time in the contributions of women to their history and society. The popularity of these books among early Christians testifies to a continuation of that interest.[24]

Women may also have played some more active role in the developing worship of the synagogues, which were swiftly spreading out into the Diaspora in Jesus' time.[25] Some women may even have enjoyed the title, "Ruler of the Synagogue."[26] Some others may have found the means to leave the organized religious life of secular families for a more austere alternative. Scattered ascetic communities flourished in the first century world of Judaism, though they did not long survive the destruction of the Jewish state. In the Hellenized atmosphere of Egypt, Philo observed communities of Jewish *Therapeutae* and suggested that they had been influenced by Greek philosophical "sects."[27] But Judaism produced other ascetic communities where there is no reason to suspect Greek influence.[28] The Essenes, who were rediscovered in the Dead Sea Scrolls in the twentieth century, were committed to extreme asceticism and physical purification. They lived together, shared a common purse, and practiced manual labor for their own support. We do not know, however, to what extent women may have been eligible to share this ideal. Pliny the Elder, a Roman observer, maintained that the Essenes had no wives but were drawn from the ranks of men tired of life.[29] Philo said that the Essenes did not take wives because of the natural defects of the female sex.[30]

However, there were women in some of the Essene communities. Josephus says that some Essene groups accepted a few members who obeyed the commandment to be fruitful and multiply. They chose women who were willing to submit to extraordinary purifications and to restrict their contacts to procreative endeavors, thus minimizing the inevitable pollution as much as possible.[31] Even Philo pointed out that the Essenes were troubled by the disruptive tendencies of women, because married men were pulled away from total involvement in the community toward the conjugal alliance.[32] The *Damascus Document* suggests that some members of the Qum'ran community were married, and the *Manual of Discipline* mentions the presence of women and children.[33] Some women were buried in the cemetery at Qum'ran. These may have been the wives of Essenes or women of particular sanctity who were given the privilege of joining the community in death if they had not already done so in life.[34]

None of the documents, however, suggest that women were welcome to join these communities as independent, celibate participants. The best that the spiritually ambitious woman might expect was to attract the attention of an ascetic man and be taken in as his partner. Nevertheless, it is possible that unattached women may have been present as widows of former members. Similarly, there must have been daughters among the children of the married members, and we cannot tell at what age they left the community. Therefore, though women in Essene communities may have found the opportunity for a more extended expression of their own ascetic ideals, the evidence suggests only that they were still subject to their husbands and responsible for the care and training of their children.[35]

Women in the world beyond the Essene communities who sought a new way of life, a different set of rules to live by, found no encouragement in the religious or secular society of the age. But the ascetic ideal that was beginning to make so strong an appeal to men in the first century must have exercised its attraction on women too, though they were generally prevented from responding to it. The emerging individualism so apparent in almost every aspect of the cultural and social life of this age had its effect on the tight-knit family structure of Israel, as it had on all the other communities of the Roman world. In the Galilee, too, old communities were breaking up, growing urbanism was disrupting the established traditions of rural communities, foreigners were thrusting themselves into crumbling social structures with their unwanted and suspicious laws and religions, and new economic and social demands were rearranging even the innermost sanctuaries of home and hearth.

In every society, a fair number of women have been dissatisfied with the restraints of marriage and the family. In the world of the first century, this group was undoubtedly swollen with women who had lost their places through no will of their own. Uncertainty, insecurity, and dissatisfaction were surely among the impulses that brought so many women out of the cities to hear the messages of desert preachers like John the Baptist and Jesus.[36]

The Testimony of Women

Christianity began with a virgin, a second Eve, whose consent to bear a divinely conceived son balanced the disobedience of our first mother. Human salvation, as presented in the New Testament, was founded on a woman as surely as human damnation once had been. The story of Mary's colloquy with the angel, followed by the miraculous conception and birth of Jesus, was meant to signify a new dispensation, a new direction for the human race. According to Luke the Evangelist, who may have known Mary in her later years, she remembered the strange events that marked her youth and laid them up in her heart. Presumably, when her son had accomplished his mission, she revealed them to her fellow disciples.

The four Gospels which record the deeds and words of Jesus in the shape of a religious testament were composed by four men who have traditionally been associated with the original Christian community.[37] Matthew may have been one of the original twelve apostles. Mark has been identified with John Mark, whose Christian mother sent him to assist in the evangelical mission of Paul. Luke also has been associated with Paul and has been credited with the authorship of the *Acts of the Apostles* as well as with his Gospel. The author of the book of John claims to be the Beloved Disciple, to whom the crucified Jesus entrusted the care of his mother.

The evangelists' work consisted of collecting and sifting through the sayings and anecdotes about Jesus which had been making the rounds among Christians for some years. Even the most rigorous believers in the absolute historical truth of their work do not doubt that the incidents and lessons included in the Gospels were selected consciously and deliberately from a larger mass of material. It took a further two centuries to sort the "canonical" collections from the "apocryphal."[38] Many people contributed their testimony to the mass of raw data that the evangelists collected.[39] There is every reason to believe that many of them were women who, like the mother of John Mark, called themselves Christians at the very outset of the gospel mission recounted in the *Acts of the Apostles.* These women were probably among those who had heard Jesus preaching and then returned home to repeat what they had seen and heard to members of their own intimate circles. The spread of the gospel message could not have been so swift had it depended only upon the work of public preachers in large population centers.

Mary was among the women who followed her son during the years of his preaching. She was one of the disciples present at the inauguration of the evangelical mission.[40] She was still alive and her testimony was available to the authors of the New Testament. She remains, therefore, one of the many women whose experiences were most likely to have been incorporated into that document. It would certainly have been strange if the writers of the Gospels had presented stories involving Mary's participation in her son's mission of which she was unaware or to which she was opposed.

When she conceived Jesus, Mary was indisputably a virgin in the old sense of the word; that is, she was an unmarried woman. In that respect, she was the first of the women around Jesus who carried an aura of marginality, of suspicion, of rejection. The scandals surrounding the birth of Jesus, which Matthew's version of the story were designed to allay, outlived her: the critics of Christianity were still repeating them well into the next century,[41] even though Mary

was married by the time of Jesus' birth and her reputation as a virtuous matron salvaged. Thereafter, she probably lived an ordinary
life with her husband, raising Jesus with his brothers and sisters.[42]

Whatever the truth of Mary's past, she was the first to have
reason to emphasize the special, supernatural qualities that set her
son apart from other men. The evangelists, too, were interested in
the virgin birth only as a sign of the divinity of Jesus. Matthew was
principally interested in claiming that it fulfilled an old prophecy
that a virgin would disrupt the order of nature by bearing a son who
would usher in a new era in human history. Luke, who included the
stories of the annunciation by the angel, Mary's visit to Elizabeth,
and the most detailed narrative of the birth of Jesus, was attempting
to work out a post-resurrection Christological theory demonstrating
the simultaneous humanity and divinity of Jesus. Thus, the gospels
do not praise Mary's virginity for its own sake, but only as a guaran-
tor of the divinity of her son.

It was only in later ages that Mary's virginity became the center
of a cult. The gospels give no indication that she was interested in
the exemplary possibilities of her own life except as a model of obedience to God's commands. Indeed, they suggest that she was
prepared to subordinate even the claims of her maternity to the advancement of Jesus' mission. In her later years, she may well have
collaborated in the creation of that literary Jesus who possesses
almost no human background. It is, in fact, in the gospel of John,
the evangelist who claims to have taken her into his care, that all
trace of Jesus' birth and early life are most completely obscured in
favor of an eschatalogical birth on the occasion of his baptism by
John the Baptist.[43]

Similarly, the gospels give an impression of estrangement between Jesus and his mother that is hardly borne out by her continued
presence in his entourage. John reports that Mary and Jesus'
brothers accompanied him to Capernaum.[44] There he parted from
them. Luke says he lost them in the crowds.[45] Mark suggests that
they had left him and later came back to try to persuade him to give
up his preaching and return home.[46] All three of the synoptic
gospels, Matthew, Mark, and Luke, record his answer: "Who is
my mother and who are my brothers? . . . here are my mother and
my brothers! For whoever does the will of my Father in Heaven is
my mother and sister and brother."[47]

Like everything else in the Gospels, this story intention is not
simply to provide biographical data. Rather, it dramatically il-

lustrates the allegiance Jesus felt for the eschatalogical family, bound by faith rather than biology or secular society.[48] Here Jesus demonstrated the rejection of earthly ties that he would later urge upon his aspiring followers. At least some members of his human family must have made a similar recasting of their relationships with him, for they remained among his disciples until his death and after.[49] Except for a single mention by John, we know nothing about Jesus' sisters,[50] but at least one of his brothers was active in his following, became head of the church in Jerusalem, and was one of the first to die for the new faith. Mary was still among his followers when he died and remained with them, at least for a while.

In her middle years, Mary was joined by other women who shared the conviction that her son had a unique and important message for them. These women are among the sources behind the sources for the life of Jesus: they were among the original witnesses from whose testimony the Gospels were drawn. The Gospels mention many women who heard Jesus' teaching and would have preserved the memory of their experience after his death. Moreover, many of the women mentioned in the *Acts of the Apostles* and the Pauline letters were active evangelists. Their preaching must have conveyed the sympathy they found in him for women caught in the shadows cast by the unyielding social architecture of the ancient world. They represent an active tradition, therefore, which must have been known to the evangelists and surely found its place in the construction of the literary Jesus, the permanent form of the man passed down to posterity.

Unfortunately for the historian, the Gospels have a sporadic, disjointed character. Individuals emerge and recede from the multitudes who followed Jesus around the countryside only as it suits the theological purposes of the authors. Indeed, only a few of the twelve apostles themselves are singled out in the course of the narratives. If, therefore, this account of the women among the disciples appears at times disjointed and uncertain, it is not much less so than an account of the men around Jesus would have to be.

For the sake of convenience, the women who appear in the gospels as active participants in the mission of Jesus can be divided into three groups: (1) those who appear as the partners or dependents of men in his following; (2) women who are the beneficiaries of miracles; (3) women who pursued an active discipleship and who can be counted as among the first Christians.

Only a few women relatives of the apostles had occasion to

become the centers of an event deemed suitable for inclusion in the Gospels. The first of these was Peter's mother-in-law. When Jesus visited her house, she was suffering from a fever which prevented her from entertaining him. Jesus cured her.[51] The record does not go on to tell us whether she remained at home thereafter or joined Peter and the others in following him. The gospels are also silent on the subject of Peter's wife. Presumably, she heard Jesus speak when he was in their home. We do not know whether or not she accompanied her husband during the time that he travelled about the countryside with Jesus. After Jesus' death, however, she did accompany her husband on his missionary journeys.[52]

Apocryphal tradition also preserved the belief that Peter had a daughter who lived with him in his later years. Indeed, she may have been the first proponent of virginity as a special way of life. There is a story to this effect dating at least from the second century. When one of her suitors became so importunate that she could not discourage him by conventional means, she turned to God, who intervened miraculously to strike her down with a debilitating illness. Determined to retain her virginity throughout her life, she decided, after consulting with her father, that the safest course would be to continue to suffer the disease that had saved her. She did not relent in her intention even after her disappointed suitor converted to Christianity. According to this story, Peter could cure her at will: he had her rise and walk about the room before returning, a cripple, to her couch. In this manner, they both confirmed the voluntary nature of her sacrifice. In the later Roman tradition of the fourth century, she was venerated as Petronilla, a virgin martyr.[53]

The sons of Zebedee also joined Jesus in Galilee, leaving their father in his fishing boat.[54] Their mother apparently also left Zebedee, at least for intermittent periods, to travel in their company. On one occasion, she gave Jesus the cue for a lesson in humility by denying her request that he place her sons first among the apostles in heaven.[55] Later on, she was among the women from Galilee who were with Jesus when he died.[56]

Jesus' entourage also included a number of women who were there independently of men. The evangelists often noted them as representative of the humble folk, the marginal people to whom Jesus' mission was so markedly addressed. The cure of a crippled woman, for example, provoked the charge from Jesus' enemies that he was breaking the rules of the Sabbath.[57] Jesus' sympathy with the plight of widows, so often illustrated in his parables, inspired one of the few accounts in which he is said to have raised the dead.[58] Despite his extreme reluctance to share his ministry with Gentiles, Jesus could not resist the pleas of a Canaanite woman to cure her daughter.[59] It is not very likely that any of those women returned home without first spending some time with Jesus, acquainting themselves with his history and his teaching. It is even less likely that on their return they failed to spread the news of his deeds among all who would listen to them.

Jesus associated with and aided many outcast women, but few as universally shunned as the woman who waylaid him on his way to raise the "daughter of a ruler of the Synagogue" from the dead. This woman, who had been suffering from a flow of blood for twelve years, had crept out of the crowd to seize his robe surreptitiously and steal the healing power from him.[60] In Jewish law, a menstruating woman was in a severe state of pollution. She could not share her husband's bed nor eat at table with him nor even touch his food (unless there was absolutely no other woman available to do the cooking). The life of a woman in a permanent state of hemorrhage must have been as intolerable as that of a leper. The woman who was healed of such a disability must have told her tale far and wide. It made its way into all three synoptic gospels. Moreover, in the apocryphal tradition, she appeared at Jesus' trial in Jerusalem, attempting to give favorable testimony for him even in that hostile court.[61] In that version, she was driven out unheard because the judges refused to accept the testimony of a woman. Indeed, the same woman was to enjoy further fame in the Christian tradition. She appears in second century accounts as "Berenice," a name she may have acquired in confusion with Berenice, the wife of Herod, who was also present at Jesus' trial. Under the Roman form of the name, Veronica, she has been informally canonized as the woman who wiped Jesus' face with her veil and received its imprint as a reward.

Another group of women appear in the New Testament as followers of Jesus in a more active capacity. The first of these, after his mother, was the Samaritan woman whom he converted at Jacob's well. She was not physically disabled, but was, nonetheless, an outcast, for she belonged to a nation held in peculiar disdain by Jesus' contemporaries. The disciples, who must have been hardened to some of Jesus' peculiar ways by that time, were, nevertheless, shocked when they found him in earnest conversation with such a woman. Moreover, she had a rather dubious personal background. When she told Jesus that she was unmarried, he replied: "You are right in saying, 'I have no husband.' For you have had five husbands and he whom you have now is not your husband.'' Nevertheless, according to John, Jesus singled her out as the first person to be told that he was the Messiah in whose coming she had proclaimed her ardent faith.[62]

Thus, in the Gospel of John, and only in John, a woman was the first to recognize Jesus' mission—a primacy attributed to Peter in the three synoptic Gospels.[63] This presents something of a puzzle. If John's Gospel was written before the others, it would appear that the authors of the later books objected to the story and transferred the recognition scene to Peter (along with the promise of the keys to the kingdom of heaven upon which the clerical hierarchy bases its authority). Or, recognizing it as a conflicting story, they simply omitted it from their versions. If the traditional opinion which gives chronological precedence to the synoptics is correct, it may be that the ''Beloved Disciple'' was making a subtle and deeply ironic criticism of Peter's claim.[64]

As I have already noted, the Samaritan woman undertook a successful evangelical mission among her fellow townspeople. Did she then abandon her lover and follow Jesus? We do not know. There is no reference to her in the other Gospels. Mark, however, introduces a woman named Salome at the Crucifixion ''who, when he was in Galilee, followed him and ministered to him.''[65] Salome plays a rather prominent role in some of the apocryphal gospels of the next century as a prophetic woman. The Gospel of Thomas, which also omitted the story of Peter's recognition of Jesus as the Christ, recounts a scene evocative of the exchange at Jacob's well:

> Jesus said: ''Two will rest on a bed; the one shall die and the other will live.''
>
> Salome said: ''Who are you, man, that you, as though from the One, have come up on my couch and eaten from my table?''
>
> Jesus said to her: ''I am He who exists from the Undivided. I was given some of the things of my father.''
>
> Salome said: ''I am your disciple.''
>
> Jesus said to her: ''Therefore, I say, if he is undivided, he will be filled with light; but if he is divided, he will be filled with darkness.''[66]

A similar ancient, but non-canonical, tradition recalled that "three women always worked with the lord: his mother, and her sister, and Magdalene who was called his companion and they were all named Mary."[67] The proliferation of women named Mary in the New Testament is indeed a cause of consternation to any student interested in sorting out the women in Jesus' entourage. Virtually nothing is now known of the second Mary, who appears only in John's account among the women at the Crucifixion: "his mother's sister, Mary the wife of Clopas."[68] She may have enjoyed some popularity in early Christian tradition, but she failed to do anything that would provoke a didactic reaction from Jesus and therefore receded into the crowd of anonymous women who surrounded him.

Mary Magdalene, the woman from Magdala, was, of course, destined for a long and sturdy life in legend. Few personages have won as much enduring popularity as she. But the references to her in the New Testament are far less colorful than her subsequent legend as a repentant prostitute and the evangelist of Narbonese Gaul. According to Luke, she was exorcized of seven demons and thereafter travelled about with Jesus, along with two other women who had also been cured of this disability: "He went preaching through the cities and villages and bringing the good news of the kingdom of God. And the twelve were with him, and also some women who had been healed of evil spirits and infirmities: Mary called Magdalene, from whom seven demons had gone out, and Joanna the wife of Chuza, Herod's steward, and Susanna, and many others who provided for them out of their means."[69] Joanna, in particular, is interesting because she was apparently still married to a very prominent man in Galilee. We do not know under what circumstances she may have come to Jesus to be relieved of diabolic possession, or why that particular group of women banded together. They might possibly have represented a special form of mission among the disciples, like the leaders of some modern ecstatic cults, for whom diabolic possession proves to be a route of escape from an intolerable domestic situation into a new position of leadership and self-expression.[70]

Yet a fourth Mary rivals the Magdalene in Christian tradition for the dubious honor of identification as the woman whom Jesus saved from stoning for adultery by the straightforward device of challenging "him who is without sin" to cast the first stone.[71] She was Mary of Bethany, sister of Martha and Lazarus, a woman who figures in no less than three highly significant evangelical events. John introduced the sisters at their home in Bethany grieving for their brother whom Jesus then raised from the dead.[72] The rest of Mary's history revolves around the supper in Bethany that preceded Jesus' final trip to Jerusalem. On that occasion, or on some earlier visit of Jesus to their home, Martha complained of Mary's neglect of her domestic duties because she was engrossed in listening to the teaching of Jesus. This provoked from him the gentle rebuke which has served ever since as a charter for women who would forsake the domestic for the contemplative life: "Martha, Martha, you are anxious about many things; one thing is needful. Mary has chosen the better part and it shall not be taken from her."[73]

Mary's choice has often been cited as a symbol of the life of virginity. But Mary appears to have been one of those penitents so powerfully drawn to Jesus: it was she who passionately annointed his feet before he set out on his last fateful journey and dried them with her unbound hair:

> Do you see this woman? I entered your house, you gave me no water for my feet, but she has wet my feet with her tears and wiped them with her hair. You gave me no kiss, but from the time I came in she has not ceased to kiss my feet. You did not anoint my head with oil, but she has anointed my feet with ointment. Therefore, I tell you, her sins, which are many, shall be forgiven, for she has loved much; but he who is forgiven little, loves little.[74]

In summary, the New Testament introduces us to an odd collection of female misfits: poor and outcast, widowed and adulterous, possessed and polluted. But they were also grateful and loving, women of spiritual aspirations and religious energy, who came up from Galilee with Jesus and who accompanied him steadfastly to the end when most of the twelve had betrayed and denied him. At least one of them had money and influence and, like "Veronica," may have made a last minute effort to save Jesus from his fate. Joanna, wife of Chuza, may well have taken advantage of the presence of Herod and his wife Berenice at Pilate's house on that fateful day to do some socializing of her own.[75] Is it possible that a word or two from her might have accounted for the abortive attempt of Pilate's wife to prevent the condemnation of Jesus on the grounds that she had had a bad dream about it?[76]

Jesus went to his death among a crowd of women "who bewailed and lamented him.'' One of them was his mother, in the care of the Beloved Disciple. Other evangelists name Mary Magdalene, Salome, and the mother of the sons of Zebedee among them.[77] These women constitute the first community of Christians. Rescued from physical infirmities and social stigma, they were among the ''despised and rejected of men.'' They had left their homes, if they had homes, and their friends in Galilee to share the hardships of his road. They emptied their purses to minister to him and his companions. Through the last tormented days, they held fast to their leader and rescued his body from the cross, and laid it in the tomb.

Two Marys,[78] Salome,[79] Joanna,[80] possibly with some other women, were the first to discover Jesus' empty tomb. The vision of the risen Christ was given first to the Magdalene who, thereby, became the first chosen apostle of the post-resurrection faith. Indeed, the other apostles did not believe her message, for which Jesus rebuked them when he appeared to them the following night at dinner.[81] As Elaine Pagels has ingeniously noted, Mark may have recorded only a portion of a longer tale. A second century *Gospel of Mary* portrays the Magdalene making her revelation unexpectedly in response to the urging of the other apostles that she share her reminiscences with them. Peter and the others react with scepticism and hostility to her claim that Jesus had risen, provoking a tearful and resentful outburst from Mary. Peace was restored only when they were reminded that, of all the apostles, Jesus had loved Mary best of all.[82]

It was not simple churlishness on the part of the apostles that moved them to reject Mary's claim. Nor was it negligence that caused the evangelists to blur and obscure the story. A whole theology of the subjection of women is based on the primacy of Adam in the order of creation. A whole church rests on the primacy of Peter, to whom Paul gave priority in the vision of the risen Christ. If the Samaritan woman preceded him in recognizing the divinity of Jesus, and the Magdalene preceded him in this second revelation, what becomes of the whole Petrine claim? Muted as the tale became in the Gospels, it often disturbed the Fathers of the Church, who wondered why a woman was thus singled out.

The answer is simple, really. It was a woman who was there when the men were gone, when even God appeared to have forsaken Jesus.

FIGURE 2. St. Petronilla leading Veneranda into Heaven. Rome, Catacomb of Domitilla.
From Grabar, André, *Early Christian Art* (New York: Odyssey Press, 1968), plate 231.

Chapter Two: True Yokemates

Christian history began when the apostles, "together with the women and Mary, the mother of Jesus, and with his brothers," received prophetic inspiration.[1] Peter rose up and preached to the text of the prophet Joel: "Your sons and your daughters shall prophesy: . . . on all my men servants and maid servants in those days I will pour out my spirit and they shall prophesy."[2] Women had been prophets in Israel from the time of Deborah. In Jesus' time, the prophetess Anna devoted her eighty-four-year widowhood to worship and prayer, haunting the Temple day and night. She was the first witness to proclaim that the baby Jesus was the Messiah "to all who were looking for the redemption of Jerusalem."[3]

At that time, however, prophets had fallen into some disrepute. Their reliance on individual inspiration and their independence of both priestly and secular power alienated both Jewish and Roman officials. Josephus noted scornfully that prophets were particularly popular with common people and with women of all ranks—in other words, with those people least attached to the constituted order.[4] It is not surprising, therefore, that we should find so many women associated with Jesus, nor that the same women continued his preaching when he was gone.

The Development of the Gospel Message

Initially, the women who were with Jesus when he died, both those from Galilee and the "daughters of Jerusalem," were among the missionaries of his faith. During the weeks after Pentecost, their numbers were swollen by numerous converts who responded to the preaching in Jerusalem.[5] We do not know the exact content of this early mission. Most of the people who would have heard the apostles and their friends preach in Jerusalem just after Pentecost were probably already familiar with some elements of Jesus' life and preaching. Therefore, the central message would have concentrated on the news of his resurrection and continued mission of salvation and on the warning that dominated his later sermons, that the end of the world was near. For a time, the first Christians took little heed for their future and even demanded that converts sell their property and contribute the proceeds to a common purse.[6] Soon, however, the immediacy of the second coming began to recede. Christians began to retain their homes, where they offered communal meals to disciples after their daily attendance at the Temple.[7] The group that had been drawn to Jerusalem by Jesus and their converts began to break up; some of them sold everything and set out to carry the word abroad. Others, no doubt, returned to their homes where they could relate their experiences and new-found faith to their neighbors.

As a result, a loose network of people who shared the belief that Jesus was their redeemer spread from Jerusalem to most of the lands of the eastern Mediterranean. Many disciples were constantly on the move; others confined their activities to their own towns. They ate meals together when the opportunity arose and they prayed together when they could. But in no sense could they be called a "church."[8]

Only a few years after the Pentecostal visitation, there was a sufficiently impressive community in Damascus to attract the attention of Saul (later Paul). A few years later, there were large and fairly prosperous groups in cities like Corinth and Antioch. By the sixties, the community in Rome was large enough to draw notice from the Emperor Nero when he was seeking a scapegoat for the great fire that had destroyed a substantial part of the city. But elsewhere, as suggested in a letter attributed to Clement of Rome at the end of the first century, a single Christian—and that one a woman—might constitute the whole of the community.[9]

Whoever they were, wherever they were, they bore witness. A message began to take shape that began with the story of Mary, the second Eve, who lifted the curse of the first Eve and brought a new world into being. Female evangelists contributed their memories and experiences to the making of that story, as it was repeated and transmitted to a new generation of listeners. Naturally, no one can claim to have a secret key for separating gospel material with a feminine origin from that with a masculine origin. Yet, in one sense, at least, women were active collaborators in the writing of these books. The gospels, or that oral tradition from which they were constructed, reflect the teaching heard in early Christian assemblies, a teaching that can hardly have been uniform. All the witnesses to Jesus' life must have been questioned repeatedly and the contradictions in their stories heatedly discussed. The elusive, mysterious words of Jesus and their application to the ever-recurring themes of daily life had to be sifted and interpreted with passionate conviction. Though we cannot accurately distinguish the voices of women, it is unmistakably clear that the Gospels deliberately address auditors of both genders. The homely examples that underscore Jesus' preaching were drawn from the experiences of women as well as of men. Occasionally they were artfully paired, as when the story of the good shepherd rejoicing over the recovery of the lost sheep is balanced by the story of the diligent housewife rejoicing because she found the coin she had lost from her savings.[10] This style reflects a living interchange between the teacher and his pupils, a direct tie between ethical principles and the lives of their practitioners.

Inevitably, the process of formulating a gospel tradition to which the entire Christian community could subscribe involved much discussion and debate, setting splinter groups against one another as surely as the interpretations of such latter-day prophets as Marx and Freud have splintered and stimulated their followers. Many of the traditions discarded by the early Christians have been lost, but some survive in the fragmentary remains of quasi-orthodox apocryphal traditions recorded in later centuries; some can be gleaned from the arguments against them put forth by orthodox writers. We know, for example, that women were active among the early prophets and that their activity in the Corinthian community was even approved by Paul.[11] In the vision of John the Revelator, we have muted traces of debates in which some of the factions were led by women.[12] We can also recognize that the determination with which the compilers of the Pauline letters ordered women to be silent in church and to defer to their husbands reflected a situation in which women were doing no such thing.[13] Indeed, as we shall see, the one thing that is certain about the women of the first Christian generation is that many of them had no husbands to defer to.

The women who appeared in the Gospel stories were among those who helped to construct its message. They had known a teacher who pitted himself against a social order that forced individuals into tightly constructed niches or cast them out altogether. The institutions that excluded the female disciples, the magnates that ignored them, Caesar and Caesar's world, the Temple and its priesthood, were relegated to an outer sphere of darkness. Reversing the hierarchy of their world, Jesus drew the outcasts into his own inner circle and promised them first place in his kingdom.

The injustices suffered by widows were especially apparent to Jesus. When he wished to explain the reversal of roles and conditions which would characterize his kingdom, he compared it to God's preference for the widow's mite, given from meager resources in the true spirit of charity, over the self-congratulatory largesse of the wealthy. To be sure, the widow, forlorn and helpless, is a stereotype in many literatures. But Jesus actively and publicly denounced the scribes who "devour the houses of widows" through legal devices in words that must have resonated in the ears of their victims.[14] Those widows, and most other women, were excluded from the public world of judges and pharisees whom Jesus scorned. When he told them that the letter of the law was murderous, many women had good reason to agree. When Jesus urged his followers to besiege God like an importunate widow against an indifferent judge, they must have responded with a warm rush of recognition.[15]

Jesus commended the internal virtues as opposed to the public virtues of the classical world: the feelings of sorrow, charity, and compassion which flourished beyond the world of law courts and markets. To persons whom society had already humbled, persecuted, cast out in hunger and bereavement, Jesus offered dignity and self-confidence. He validated their experience by claiming that they were to inherit the celestial kingdom which he represented. They remembered him and, when he was gone, they helped to keep that memory alive for others.

The author of the *Acts of the Apostle*, our only narrative record concerning the first Christian generation, recorded only a few of the discussions that agitated the community leaders as they sought to determine which of the ancient divine laws of the Old Testament they would retain and which they would discard as they formulated a distinctively Christian way of life. The arguments over dietary laws and male circumcision cannot have been the only confrontations they endured. We know that they also discarded the rituals of female purification which emphasized the biological differences between women and men and contributed to the social construction of women as beings on a different and inferior level of creation. When Jesus cured "Veronica," he said to her: "Woman thou art healed of thy infirmity."[16] The women, and also the men, who heard the story knew that her long hemorrhaging had rendered her untouchable according to the laws governing ritual purification for women after menstruation and childbirth. She was considered polluted and dangerous; she had not dared to approach Jesus openly. Yet, when he became aware of her, he did not recoil but praised her for her act of faith.

The Christians had by no means conquered the fear and revulsion that men in many cultures have felt toward the physiology of women. They had, however, de-institutionalized it by turning their backs on practices designed to convert it into a set of social taboos. Somehow, they had broadened Jesus' words to "Veronica" into a manifesto which relieved all women from the stigma of "infirmity."

More broadly, I should like to suggest that the literary representation of Jesus' personality owes a great deal to the perceptions of his female followers. The sympathy and compassion of the literary Jesus validated a set of virtues which could be positively opposed to the traditional manliness so admired in the ancient world. Where the very word "virtue" is built on the root, *vir* or man, the positive aspects of male strength seem to have no counterpart but female weakness.[17] Insofar as women were simply "not-man," unmanly, they lacked positive virtues of their own except the virtue of faithfully serving men.[18] Jesus, with his kindness, his condemnation of violence, and his rejection of the fruits of worldly ambition, presented a model of strength and beauty capable of emulation by women as well as men. His likeness to women and his compatibility with women were, perhaps, embedded in the record of the gospel by enthusiastic devotees enjoying the first of the successive periods of "feminization" which have recurred throughout Christian history.[19]

The gospel record not only delineates a set of virtues which turn the female experiences of powerlessness, humility, and poverty into positive models, but it commemorated a series of bitter attacks which Jesus made on the institutions of the patriarchal family, which defined and enforced the functional roles of women as daughters, wives, and mothers. In the ancient societies of the Mediterranean, the family was the foundation of the body politic and the father was the juridical and moral head of the family. No individual could expect to acquire status, wealth, or power outside its confines. For men, marriage and paternity opened the way to the adult responsibilities of the public world. For women, marriage and maternity were the only acceptable roles. Those who failed at either were reduced to the quasi-domestic functions of servants, concubines, or dependent widows. Outside their familial settings such women had no recognized existence at all.

We have noted that many of Jesus' female followers came from this shadowy half-world. The message they preached later, through the gospels, was hostility to the social and political centrality of the

family and to all the institutions that smothered the living spirit.
They repeated the endorsement of Jesus of the concept of marriage,
not as an authoritarian institution, but as a conjugal union. Ignoring
centuries of tradition, Jesus based his view of marriage on a for-
tuitous and virtually forgotten text in Genesis: "Therefore, a man
leaves his father and mother and cleaves to his wife, and they
become one flesh."[20]

This ideal conforms neither to the polygynous tradition of
Judaism nor to the Roman tradition of serial monogamy. It flouts the
universal tradition that marriages are made by fathers in the interests
of the larger family unit. Moreover, Jesus prohibited divorce, making an exception only for "fornication." Nor did he say whose fornication he meant. Later church councils were repeatedly forced to
consider the possibility that men, too, might be considered guilty of
adultery. Formerly, the laws of every city or state in the Mediterranean world charged men with adultery only as the accomplices of
married women. What must have been the effect upon the listening
women when Jesus said that a man who leaves his wife and marries
another is an adulterer?[21] How often did they repeat to everyone
who would listen the tale of his rescue of the woman taken in
adultery? The old law uncompromisingly commanded that she be
stoned to death. Jesus commanded only that she go and sin no
more.[22]

His attack on the loyalties and responsibilities of family life went
further than a simple display of compassion for the endangered. We
have already noted his public and uncompromising relegation of his
mother and brothers to a simple place among those who obeyed the
word of God. On another occasion, when a woman in the crowd
cried out, "Blessed is the womb that bore thee and the breasts that
gave thee suck," Jesus answered, "Blessed rather are those who
hear the word of God and keep it."[23] The incorporation of these incidents in the gospels reflects a clear understanding among their
compilers that Jesus was expressing something more than personal
irritation with his own family. The presence of his mother among
the disciples seems clearly to indicate that, in fact, he did not reject
her. But he redefined their relationship to a simple individual attach-
ment, independent of the accidents of biology. His notion that
adherence to the word of God was sufficient to bring his followers
together in a familial relationship with him tended to cut individuals
away from the roles that their chance physical and social fortunes
had imposed upon them.[24]

Thus, the heart of Jesus' message centered on the uninhibited, direct relationship of a person with a "heavenly father." Intermediaries of every social and domestic rank were swept away. In heaven, there was to be no marriage or giving in marriage.[25] Against the claims of earthly patriarchs, Jesus advanced the authority of God, counselling his followers not even to delay to bury their earthly fathers: "let the dead bury the dead."[26]

Considering the minimal role which women were allotted in first-century Judaism, his female listeners may have been confronted with an entirely novel proposition in the idea that they could address God directly.[27] It may well have seemed to them that he had healed them of spiritual infirmities as surely as he had healed "Veronica" of her physical infirmity. The first generation of Christian women knew that they had souls capable of salvation, souls which drew sustenance from Mary's choice of the better part. Jesus was preaching revolt. He was urging, not the overthrow of the irrelevant political order of Caesar, but of the far more fundamental domestic order of the patriarchal family:

> Do not think that I have come to bring peace on earth! I have not come to bring peace but a sword. For I have come to set a man against his father and a daughter against her mother and daughter-in-law against mother-in-law and a man's foes will be those of his own household. He who loves father or mother more than me is not worthy of me. He who finds his life shall lose it and he who loses his life for my sake shall find it.[28]

In the centuries to come, daughters, mothers, and wives would not be slow to heed those words. Many of them would leave all and follow after him. And, as Jesus had predicted, they would be persecuted and their own relatives would deliver them up to death. But the women who spread the news of Jesus also remembered that "anyone who leaves houses or brothers or sisters or father or mother or children or lands for my name's sake will receive back a hundred fold."[29]

The Apostolic Sisterhood

Some of the rhetoric of the New Testament encourages the speculation that the first Christians made an attempt to introduce egalitarian principles into their common lives and to isolate themselves as far as possible from the institutions of the stratified Roman world.[30] The process of spreading the word depended only in part on a charismatic leadership: the restrictions of gender and status roles were cast aside in light of the urgency of the work that each convert was called upon to do. While only the apocryphal traditions excluded from the final redaction of the New Testament retained memories of the later lives of some of Jesus' female companions and most of the apostles, we may be sure that first-century Christians were always ready to give special attention to anyone who had been an eyewitness to Jesus' life and works.

The only way in which we can adequately explain the speed and breadth of the expansion of Christianity in the first century is to envisage each convert as the potential center of a new community. Even in the larger cities, where frequent communication remained possible, Christians probably split quickly into small groups, each advancing a special social and religious vision governed only by a common memory of Jesus' preaching. Thus, there was room for groups in which women might lay claim to egalitarian goals and where they might even have sought an androgynous life-style.[31] Moreover, many members of this generation which believed in the imminent end of the world, may have readily rejected the special procreative role of women in favor of a less gender-defined commitment to the future kingdom. Women seeking new definitions of their value and mission probably enlisted men who supported their spiritual claims but were troubled and divided about their implications on earth. Other men, and women too, must have repudiated such innovations with appeals to the moral traditions of the Old Testament.

Some married couples simply entered the Christian community together and took up a new evangelical partnership. Some of the apostles were married and took their wives with them on their travels. Paul says plainly that Cephas (Peter) and other apostles travelled with their wives, though he himself did not do so. The community supported these families wherever they went, though Paul suggests that they may have complained about it.[32] Whether or not Peter took his mother-in-law and his daughter with him is less clear. These apostolic couples may have radically changed their relationships to one another as a result of their peripatetic missions. They may have suspended conjugal relations both for purposes of ritual purity and to avoid being hampered by children in their migratory lives.[33]

Paul briefly recorded the names of couples who worked together as laborers in the vineyards of the Lord. First among them were Priscilla and Aquila, whom he met first in Corinth where they housed him for a year and a half.[34] Later, they went with him to Ephesus where they remained when Paul went on to Macedonia. In Ephesus, they encountered Apollos who had already been baptized by John and had begun to preach the word of Jesus. They undertook to instruct him "more accurately" before sending him on to Paul. The couple apparently migrated from Ephesus to Rome, where Paul sent them greetings at a later date.[35] The Roman church also produced Linus and Claudia.[36] Finally, Paul greeted Junia and Andronicus, "outstanding among the apostles."[37]

Not all these husband and wife teams travelled as missionaries. Many of them, for one reason or another, were not inclined to break with their roots or give up all their property, despite the unhappy biblical example of Ananias and Sapphira, who were miraculously struck dead for their refusal to part with everything.[38] Many married couples who appear in later records kept their houses and sufficient portions of their incomes to give ready hospitality to Paul and other itinerant preachers. Indeed, the "house churches" maintained throughout the growing Christian world were the foundations of the new religion.[39]

As permanent Christian communities became established, a clerical group of bishops and deacons emerged to minister to them. Paul expected the bishops to prove themselves as responsible husbands and fathers before undertaking the care of a community.[40] Deaconesses shared the work of deacons and many may have been their wives. No doubt these apostolic wives devoted themselves principally to the physical functions of keeping their husbands fit for preaching and performing miracles. But they also must have shared in the missionary work itself, if only in the informal capacity of spreading the word among women in the communities they visited. Later on, Clement of Alexandria, the staunch defender of marriage against the rising fashion of virginity, noted Paul's insistence that bishops and deacons be tested on their ability to run a harmonious household.[41] Clement claimed that the apostles' wives were evangelists to women in their households, just as their husbands were to men in public.[42] He also related the beautiful tale of the martyrdom of Peter's wife, consoled and encouraged by her husband to the end.[43]

Naturally not every married woman who was moved to believe in the risen Jesus was converted jointly with her spouse. In the first generation, and for centuries to come, the problem of the relations of Christians married to non-Christians plagued the community. The conflict probably caused some wives to leave their husbands and cast themselves on the Christian community if they did not have sufficient private means to support themselves. But we should not discount the probability that a number of women of means took advantage of the easy access to divorce offered by Roman law to separate from their non-Christian husbands. They could have used their funds to support other members of their new-found community.

Paul advised against divorce for those whose partners were amenable to continuing the marriage, "for the unbelieving husband is consecrated through his wife."[44] But he readily accepted the reality of broken marriages between such partners. Thus, a number of the women whose marital status is unknown to us probably were living in chaste separation from their husbands as the result of religious conflict.

These may account for the women who are mentioned as the primary converters of their own children. Even before Paul had begun his mission, Mary, the mother of John Mark, was educating her son for a future of preaching and writing the first of the synoptic gospels.[45] In Lystra, Asia Minor, a Christian woman named Eunice, with the help of her own Christian mother, Lois, raised the young Timothy, whom Paul would take with him on his later missions.[46] It is no wonder, then, that Paul should have cautioned Timothy not to enroll women in the order of widows until they had discharged their duty to their children and grandchildren.[47]

Although these apostolic women performed roles in the new church that transcended their familial functions, they remained fixed in the traditional social structure. The New Testament, however, took notice of some women who appear to have moved altogether outside their allotted roles. A few women are presented as participants in the life of the church who had no apparent attachments to men or to families. Their appearance as independent beings contributed to a new social architecture which would provide a special place for the unmarried woman.

In the New Testament, the only explicitly unmarried women are widows. Paul, in fact, speaks of widows as an "order" whose membership must be restricted to a chosen few.[48] It may well be that the inspiration and model for such an order came from Mary herself. The total disappearance of Joseph from the New Testament record has traditionally been explained as a result of his death early in Jesus' life. When Mary appears in the Gospels, she is usually part of a group of women attending Jesus. According to Luke, her life was an apostolate that began when she submitted to the divine commandments relayed by the angel and culminated in her presence at the pentecostal gathering. Mary, he said, remembered everything and pondered it all in later years. I have already suggested that she collaborated actively in the biblical subordination of her maternal claims to special consideration from Jesus to the greater claim of the eschatalogical family of believers.[49]

Luke's *Acts of the Apostles,* which placed Mary among the post-Resurrection community in Jerusalem, suggests that widows were already perceived as a group defined by qualities beyond the simple loss of a husband. The altercation which arose because the "hellenists" believed that "their widows were neglected in the daily distributions" by the Hebrews, is difficult to interpret in the context of a community that boasted of sharing everything in common.[50] Granted, widows may appear to be more vulnerable and in need of support than men or married people. But no mention is made here of people who must have had similar claims, such as orphans, the sick, the aged or any others among the destitute. Perhaps, along with the apostles, widows had already been designated as a special and privileged group within the community, worthy of its full support, as opposed to others who were expected to earn money for the common fund.[51] The "hellenists" were probably Greek-speaking Jews from outside Judaea, who perhaps felt discriminated against by those who came from Jerusalem.

When Luke wrote the *Acts of the Apostles,* he may have taken it for granted that his readers were familiar with the order of widows mentioned by Paul. He had accompanied Paul on some of his missionary voyages and was therefore acquainted with Paul's methods of church organization, which may or may not have conformed to those of the Jerusalem church. Paul took it for granted that widows of every age and condition must be supported if they had been left destitute. But he stipulated that the need for support did not qualify them for membership among the "true widows." We do not know whether this group was already a distinct component of the community in Jerusalem, but by the end of the first apostolic generation, the "order" was widespread and the restrictions formulated by Paul (or whoever wrote the first letter to Timothy in his name) were generally applied to candidates for admission. "True widows" had to be at least sixty years old; they had to have completed their childbearing years, and discharged their obligations to their grown children. In short, they had to be old enough and free enough to warrant breaking the ties that held them to family and community. Only then could they take formal vows of chastity and devote themselves to good works and constant prayer. In this sense, therefore, true widowhood transcended the accidental state of bereavement and became a voluntary condition embraced by a chosen few.

Many of the women mentioned in the *Acts of the Apostles* or in the Pauline letters seem to have transcended their social placement in the eyes of the evangelist. The traditional classifications—married, widowed, or spinster—were not relevant to their performance of the gospel mission. We do not know, for example, how Tabitha, a seamstress of Joppa, came to be a Christian or how she established and governed the community of her disciples who mourned her when she died full of good works and charity.[52] After giving expression to their grief and showing everyone the coats and garments she had made for them while she lived, they sent word to Peter who was nearby, in Lydda. He hurried to Joppa, raised her from the dead, and restored her to the widows and saints of the city. After some days, he left, presumably satisfied that the community was in good hands. Tabitha may have been a widow; she could have been an unmarried virgin.

When Saul began his house-to-house search for Christians in Jerusalem, many of the community fled to Samaria and then to more distant places. Among them was Philip, "the evangelist, one of the seven (deacons), who had four unmarried daughters who prophesied."[53] Though no one made their virginity a requirement for their prophetic status, the stress laid on their condition here strengthens the idea that virginity was already in vogue among early Christian women, and that the unmarried condition may have endowed them with a charisma that women subject to husbands lacked. Those four daughters were remembered by later Christians who traced them to Asia Minor, a province later noted for its prophetesses.[54]

At Philippi, Paul preached to a group of women who met at a "place of prayer" near the river. A women who sold purple goods from Thyatira, named Lydia, heard him and was baptized along with her entire household. Her home became the center for the church in Philippi.[55] Lydia, who commanded a household in her own right, must have been an unmarried woman. Perhaps she was one of those freedwomen who, in the early Roman Empire, could amass fortunes and undertake business ventures of their own.[56] If so, she was a worthy predecessor of the great ladies of later times whose conversion automatically netted a whole congregation of their dependents.

Apparently Paul followed the strategy of converting prominent women whenever he could. After preaching in Thessalonica, he converted some Jews, many Greeks, and "not a few of the leading women."[57] Likewise in Beroea, he converted "not a few Greek women of high standing as well as men."[58] In Athens, the woman named Damaris was converted with Dionysius the Areopagite and others.[59] These women, with their thriving households, were in a position to lay the foundation of permanent churches in the young communities. Their houses could accommodate preachers and offer a place for common meals and prayers until the community had grown sufficiently to support some more public place of worship. Thus Paul greeted Nympha in Collossus and "the church in her house."[60]

At Corinth, Paul corresponded with a woman named Chloe, whose "people" reported to him that quarrels and difficulties broke out in that church after he left.[61] He commended Phoebe, deacon of the church of Cencrae, to the Roman community as one deserving of their help because of the aid she had given him and many others.[62] Also at Rome, he greeted the mother of Rufus; Julia, the sister of Nereus; Olympas; Tryphaena and Tryphosa, "working in the Lord"; and Persis, "who had worked hard in the lord." None of these women had husbands in evidence. Finally, from his prison, he addressed an appeal to his "true yokemate" to reconcile the quarrels of two women, Evodia and Syntiche, who "have labored side by side with me in the gospel with Clement and the rest of my fellow workers."[63]

Social Innovations in the Pauline Communities

What was the quarrel that Paul urged his "true yokemate" to settle? We will never know. Perhaps it concerned innovations in sexual commitments which apparently were being discussed in the communities where he preached. We do not know much about the content of Paul's preaching at this time, although the letters indicate that it was very different from his writings. Later, in the apocryphal

tradition, he was known as an apostle of virginity and his friend
Tryphaena was associated with that teaching.[64] A world in which
men were forbidden to commit adultery and women were chosen for
the first revelations of Jesus' divinity, was a world without compass
or rudder to men of Paul's generation.

Paul himself was a man of divided mind, struggling to com-
prehend the abrupt revelations which had once been forced into his
unwilling, Pharisaic consciousness on the road to Damascus. His
surviving letters represent his attempts to resolve frictions and con-
flicts among his converts, the nature of which is rarely elucidated.
Moreover, no modern scholar now believes that Paul actually wrote
all the Pauline letters; in fact, his more reactionary commandments
on the subjection of women have been rejected as interpolations of
the next generation.[65] In any case, our concern is with the community he addressed; the Paul who envisioned a new dispensation where
there would be neither male nor female had also to deal with a living
community in which women were moving beyond the limitations of
their traditional roles.[66]

Paul's most complete missive on the questions of the relationships
between women and men and on marriage and celibacy was his first
letter to the Corinthians, which is generally conceded to be a genuine Pauline document. The church of Corinth was one of his first
implantations, and he kept in touch with his many followers there
throughout the later period of his travels. Possibly the Corinthians
had been stirred up by the ideas of Apollos. We do not know what he
was preaching before Priscilla and Aquila undertook to correct him.
In any case, some members of the community were apparently ex-
perimenting with a variety of new life-styles which leant unexpected
latitude to Paul's concept of Christian liberty. Confronted with these
innovations and the arguments they engendered, a woman named
Chloe sent some of "her people" to Paul with a report and questions
which have been lost to us. Paul's answer provides us with the first
indication that perpetual virginity was being promulgated as a
possibility among the believers in Corinth.

Paul began his letter to the Corinthians by reminding the community that they were still subject to conventional sexual standards.
One man who apparently thought that Christianity had freed him
from Roman and Jewish incest prohibitions was ordered to stop living with his father's wife.[67] Paul also confirmed traditional prohibitions against other forms of sexual activity outside of marriage.[68]
We know that heterodox communities of the second and third cen-

turies sometimes entertained the idea that the coming of the Holy Spirit freed them from constraints formerly laid on the flesh, but Paul was quick to prevent similar notions from taking root among his followers.

Paul next turned to the great question of marital relations. Like Jesus, he espoused a view of marriage as an emotional and physical relationship between two people, with no reference to parents, property rights, the claims of ancestors, progeny or the state. His view reinforced Jesus' indifference to broader community claims over individual preferences. In addition Paul suggested that at its most intimate heart marriage was to be egalitarian among Christians:

> Now, concerning the matters about which you wrote. It is well for a man not to touch a woman but because of the temptation to immorality each man should have his own wife and each woman her own husband. The husband should give to his wife her conjugal rights and likewise the wife to her husband. For the wife does not rule over her own body, but the husband does; likewise the husband does not rule over his own body, but the wife does. Do not refuse one another except perhaps by agreement for a season, that you may devote yourselves to prayer; but then come together again, lest Satan tempt you through lack of self-control. I say this by way of concession, not of command. I wish that all were as I am myself. But each has his own special gift from God, one of one kind and one of another.[69]

It appears that Paul's defense of marriage was a response to someone else's rejection of it, though we don't know whether those persons were women or men, married or celibate. Though Paul himself was apparently leading a celibate life at the time, he was clearly doubtful about the advisability of making a rule of it. He ends with a cautious endorsement for those who saw sexual renunciation as a possible alternative to marriage. His caution can be explained by the novelty of the idea, especially since no structured community like the Essenes was envisaged to discipline the celibate, and because he was endorsing celibacy at the very period when the Roman Emperors were attempting to legislate compulsory marriage for all Roman citizens.[70]

Paul also felt that he had to reinforce Jesus' demands for permanent monogamy. He thus counselled that wives should not separate from their husbands, nor husbands divorce their wives.[71] When he talked about those who were not married, however, he relaxed somewhat and, it is worth remarking, he seemed more optimistic about women celibates than men:

> . . . to the unmarried and the widows, I say that it is well for them to remain single as I do. But if they cannot exercise self-control, they should marry. For it is better to marry than to be aflame with lust.[72]

> . . . A wife is bound to her husband as long as he lives. If the husband dies she is free to be married to whom she wishes, only in the Lord. But, in my judgment, she is happier if she remains as she is. And I think that I have the Spirit of God.[73]

Were the women of Corinth (perhaps Chloe herself) leaving their husbands, claiming that the descent of the spirit had freed them from carnal commitments? Perhaps they were. In later centuries, when the ascetic movement had finally come into its own, that was not an uncommon reaction for converted women. It was a pattern, moreover, woven into the great body of inspirational literature produced in the second century. The women Paul addressed had rarely chosen their own husbands and had little control over their lives under the power of those husbands. In cases where a wife converted to Christianity and her husband did not, she may well have believed that her new religion entitled her to break the old ties. Why else did Paul feel that he had to make a judgment which did little more than reaffirm what Jesus had already said and what social custom generally indicated in any case?

His advice to the unmarried, however, was radical and innovative and has the tone of consent to an existing condition rather than a new commandment. Paul began, truthfully, by admitting that "concerning the unmarried, I have no command of the Lord." Nothing in the Gospels suggests the desirability of a celibate life (if we discount the prophetic words of Jesus in his last agony that the daughters of Jerusalem would one day wish that they had been barren and that their breasts had never given suck). Simply to give women the option to reject marriage was almost inconceivable. The ancient world did not even have a word for the spinster or virgin, except as it described a young woman not yet married. Jewish law provided rather detailed provisions for the placement of widows, and Roman law commanded that they marry again in all possible haste if they were of childbearing age.

In this context, I want to stress that Paul did not invent the idea and attempt to impose it on his congregation. The idea came from the Corinthian community. It was probably also circulating among congregations who did not receive any apostolic letters. Though Paul had his own personal preference, he approached the general subject very gingerly. We have seen that he was careful to reaffirm the traditional conjugal morality of the ancient world before he opened that small fissure in the social structure through which an unimaginable order of new beings might enter into society. Perhaps he would not even have ventured so far had he not felt that "the impending distress" justified extraordinary measures:

> . . . the appointed time has grown very short. From now on, let those who have wives live as though they had none . . . for the form of the world is passing away. I want you to be free from anxieties. The unmarried man is anxious about the affairs of the Lord, how to please the Lord; but the married man is anxious about worldly affairs, how to please his wife, and his interests are divided. And the unmarried woman or girl is anxious about the affairs of the Lord, how to be holy in body and spirit; but the married woman is anxious about worldly affairs, how to please her husband. I say this for your own benefit, not to lay any restraint upon you, but to promote good order and to secure your undivided devotion to the Lord.[74]

These remarks hardly constitute a manifesto for the embryonic ascetic movement. But they were fully enshrined in the New Testament, giving divine sanction, for some people, to a way of life at variance with the old prescriptions of Genesis. From that time forward, they fell upon fertile soil.

Paul's final piece of advice was probably aimed at these Corinthians, who were apparently the first experimenters in Christian asexuality. Some of them seem to have been married and some, perhaps, were in that intermediate state between betrothal and consummation common to the ancient process of marriage. Paul counselled that:

> If anyone thinks that he is not behaving properly toward his betrothed, if his passions are strong, and it has to be, let him

do as he wishes; let them marry—it is no sin. But whoever is firmly established in his heart, being under no necessity but having his desire under control, and has determined this in his heart to keep her as his betrothed, he will do well. So that he who marries his betrothed does well; and he who refrains from marriage will do better.[75]

Some scholars have interpreted this passage to mean that there were people in Corinth practicing marriage without sexual relationships, or living together unmarried in chaste restraint.[76]

Certainly, the women and men who formed one of the first Christian congregations known to us outside the gospels were engaged in a radical debate concerning the structure of their most intimate personal relationships. Some apparently attempted to practice a form of free love, others to keep themselves from marriage altogether, and still others to form a spiritual union free of physical expression. Paul condemned the first group and cautioned the rest that the ordinary sexual unions of married people were acceptable if carried on with mutual respect and affection. For the heroic few he endorsed, but did not initiate, the ideal of a life unfettered by conjugal concerns. He approved of the concept of chaste widowhood for women in particular and in a later letter he (or his interpolator) laid out the foundations for a special "order" of widows under oath to live chastely in the service of God.[77] This evidence suggests that it was not in Paul's head alone that the idea blossomed of a new community, where the old divisions and classifications would be erased and the followers of Christ would know "neither Jew nor Greek, slave nor free, male nor female."[78]

FIGURE 3. Orant called *Donna Velatio*. Rome, Catacomb of Priscilla, Cubiculum of the *Velatio*. From Grabar, André, *Early Christian Art* (New York: Odyssey Press, 1968), plate 96.

Chapter Three: Mary Laughed

In 64 AD, the city of Rome suffered one of the worst fires in its history. Excited rumors circulated among the people that arsonists, under orders from the Emperor Nero, were responsible for the destruction of their homes. To deflect these accusations from himself, the Emperor accused the Christians, who were apparently already known as an antisocial sect.[1] There was blood. There was violence. The Christian leadership, including Peter and Paul, was abruptly swept away. Women and men perished cruelly and publicly. Priscilla, Junia, and others named in the Pauline letters were in Rome; they may have been among the Christian women costumed as "Danae and Dircae" in a ghastly spectacle presented to the angry Roman people.[2]

The women of Rome were notorious among their contemporaries for the unprecedented freedom they enjoyed in the century after Augustus. In this age of crumbling social barriers women were able to gain political, economic, and sexual powers that older societies had denied them. Yet they often used their new found powers to reject the very society that had conferred them and embraced Christianity. The one certain thing we know about Christian women in the dim and troubled decades following the Neronian persecution is that their numbers grew steadily. Moreover, it was not simply the women of low degree who were willing to risk their lives for the hope of a better future in another world. About 110 AD, the Emperor Domitian executed his cousin Flavius and exiled his wife Flavia Domitilla. Two centuries later, Eusebius claimed that they had been sentenced as punishment for their conversion to Christianity.[3] Hagiographic legends, whose origins are unknown, claimed that Flavia Domitilla's conversion had been combined with a determination to retain her virginity, causing her to break her betrothal to the emperor.[4] This twin rejection of Roman religion and Roman social values became a characteristic of the literature relating to the conversion of women in the second century.

How did this connection develop in the post-Neronian generation? We shall see that it did not become the ideal of Christian men.

The few scraps of evidence that throw light on the Christian communities of this period suggest that the male leadership tended to return to more traditional family values once they had recognized that the end of the world was not imminent. I believe that the development of a cult of virginity and a structured celibate way of life was the work of women who, for a variety of reasons, could not be content with the conditions of married life in the early Roman Empire.

The Emancipated Women of Imperial Rome

Romans saw their social system as a loose alliance of powerful families. The state acted as an arbiter of differences among them. Private law was traditionally entrusted to the *pater familias*—the man in whom leadership of the *familia* and the disposal of its fortunes was vested. By imperial times, his authority over his sons had been greatly eroded by the claims and privileges of citizenship. He remained, however, unchallenged in his power over his daughters. By the end of the republic and the beginning of the empire, that power commonly continued even after he had arranged her marriage and settled her in a new household.

In any strongly structured, family-oriented society, the dual allegiance of women to their natal and conjugal families represents a contradition that must be solved by some rite or fiction.[5] In Rome, as elsewhere, a woman theoretically shifted allegiance and identity from her paternal to her conjugal household at the time of marriage. This event was marked by complicated financial and political negotiations and a certain amount of fanfare. It required a formal divorce to break the marriage. In reality, though, the woman was transferred to her husband's house but her husband frequently failed to gain jurisdiction over her and her goods.[6] As women became wealthier and as Roman political alliances became riskier, fathers grew more reluctant to commit themselves to the old-fashioned rites of marriage which involved the surrender of their daughters' hands to their husbands with *patria potestas* (paternal power) over them. In a hand-less, or *sine manu*, marriage, women were sent into their husbands' homes with dowries to support them but remained under the patriarchal jurisdiction of their fathers. In effect, the father lent, rather than gave, his daughter in marriage and he could take her out of it if and when his interests changed. Moreover, if a woman in such a marriage committed adultery, which was a capital offense, she was judged by her father rather than her offended husband. Thus, a Roman husband in a *sine manu* marriage had little control over his spouse. He had power over his children but not over their mother. Even if she cuckolded him, his only recourse might be to ask her father to punish her.[7]

This practice had a further, accidental effect on the practical condition of upper-class women: when their fathers died, they were still exempt from the authority of their husbands. To be sure, the conviction of Roman jurists that women suffer incurably from levity of mind ensured that, as perpetual children, they would have to submit to legal tutelage.[8] But, by law, their guardians could not be their husbands. As age, increasing strength of mind, and sometimes a succession of marriages took women further from the immediate power of an aging father or a guardian whose indifference and lack of natural authority made tutelage a sham, considerable numbers of women found themselves freer and stronger than women ever had been before.[9] Moreover, in the first and second centuries, Roman Law spread over the diverse cultures of the Mediterranean world. Augustus had conquered that world; the jurists of the classical period advanced the reality of his Imperium.

Poets and critics bewailed the growing freedom of Roman women as evidence of the sorry breakdown in Roman morality. The first to heed their complaint was "the Father of the Country," Augustus himself. He strove, even though it cost him the society of his only daughter, to repair the damages to the Roman social fabric of a century of anarchy.[10] In a series of laws, Augustus and his successors attempted to force the celibate to marry and propagate children. He penalized the unmarried and rewarded the fertile, granting noble women who bore three children and freedwomen who bore four the right, thereafter, to be free of tutelage in fully adult status. He strengthened the laws against adultery and strengthened the legal rights of concubines to stabilize unions whose social inequalities disqualified them as full marriages. Even widows were obligated to marry again as soon as possible. At first, Augustus had insisted on men remarrying immediately and women after a year, but angry demonstrations forced him to lengthen the period to three years for women.[11]

Augustus' efforts to enforce this legislation were not very successful, to judge by the frequency with which his successors reinforced it. Faced with the prevalence of the *sine manu* marriage, men saw little advantage in taking up the burdens and responsibilities of a

Roman *pater familias*. The law (whose precise content has been lost) appears to have assumed that women would obey their fathers. Its only known coercive clauses for women refer to widows. Later redactions, however, indicate that fathers practiced all sorts of subterfuges to avoid dowering their daughters. This must have resulted in the creation of an unprecedented group of celibate women, who may or may not have welcomed their escape from the demands of marriage.

Hitherto, Rome had not supported unmarried women, except for the rigidly controlled and restricted Vestal Virgins. They were accorded special privileges and complete legal liberty and were classed juridically among adult men for some purposes.[12] But there were only six of them at any given time and they were vowed to their posts by their fathers before reaching puberty. They were not volunteers and were not always faithful to their trust. Domitian condemned two vestals to death at about the same time that he was persecuting both Christians and the followers of Isis. Moreover, after serving thirty years, they were pensioned off and could marry if they wished.

Augustus' marriage laws were part of his program to restore republican virtue, but his efforts were about as successful as his program to restore the republic itself. They were, however, far more sincere. The salvation and reconstitution of the Roman family was a serious matter to him and to his successors. The Augustan marriage laws, in various reformulations, were consistently repeated by Roman jurists and sometimes enforced violently against women who desired to evade marriage, but did not have their fathers' support.

Second-century jurists recorded a series of efforts to make marriage more attractive to men by strengthening the position of a husband vis-à-vis his wife's father.[13] The famous doctrine of consent was introduced, basing marriage for men on their own choice and protecting a harmonious marriage from intervention by the wife's father. The provision of consent for the woman, however, was more equivocal: the phrase "consent makes the marriage" could, and probably was, read to mean the father's consent, not the bride's.[14] In any case, most Roman jurists considered the dowry the *sine qua non* of a marriage, and there could not be a dowry without an agreeable father. Only an orphaned heiress might have had the power to confer her dowry and her consent where she chose. Yet even she, if her tutelage were sufficiently relaxed, was still controlled by a state which prohibited wealthy aristocratic women from marrying men of socially unsuitable origins and restricted women of the lower ranks from marrying men of the aristocratic class. In short, though the breakdown of the Roman family, so distressing to social critics, resulted in substantially greater freedom for many women, this freedom was often balanced by the intervention of a state that specifically sought to be ''paternalistic.''

Augustan legislation also tried to limit the amount of property that women, particularly childless women, could control. But that was a futile endeavor.[15] Women earned money through a variety of enterprises, many of them highly profitable, though socially undesirable. They spent money in the marketplace, in the forum, and at the games. They were criticized for their vanity and luxury but also for their generosity to religious cults condemned by their male critics. To the disgust of male satirists, they participated in parties and literary salons.[16] Juvenal's dislike for female pedantry should not blind us to its prevalence.[17]

Like women of the *ancien régime* in Europe, the women of imperial Rome played an important part in the intellectual life of the age. And, like those women, they lived in a monarchy. The great political offices were certainly monopolized by men, as were the great bureaucratic posts, but the concentration of power in imperial hands gave great weight to the manipulative arts of patronage and influence which many women skillfully exercised. The savagery of Juvenal and his contemporaries towards women surely reflected their anger and envy at the success women were enjoying in the imperial environment.

Many of these women who had partially escaped from their husbands' control and who normally could expect to outlive their fathers, became famous in song and story for their unbridled sexuality. The Roman poets who loved them, or hated them, or suffered the pains of jealousy and desire, criticized them and praised them by turns for the profligacy of their sexual favors. Nor was the state indifferent to the sexual license of women. From Augustus on, the emperors sporadically intervened to punish adulterous women. More systematically, they used their legislative power to prevent sexual license from developing into marital license. The freedom of Roman women, particularly upper-class women, was restricted at two crucial points: they could not marry whomever they please if it would result in the pollution of aristocratic lineages; nor could they refuse to marry at all or to play their part in the reproduction of the Roman nobility.

Needless to say, women of the lower classes were even more firmly restricted. The Roman *familia* included slaves and other dependents who worked on estates of the *pater familias*. Through a variety of legal fictions and accommodations, his patriarchal authority also extended to a clientele embracing former slaves who had been emancipated, persons of lower status or provincial origin who enjoyed his patronage and protection, and poor people who received charity in exchange for personal or political services. The *pater familias* had a flexible degree of power over all these persons, ranging from loosely exercised patronage to the severely defined power of life and death over his children and slaves.

Daughters and slaves were physically subject to this paternal power for life and sustenance. Freedwomen generally continued to depend on their former masters for protection and influence, though they could dispose freely of their own property and enter into commercial enterprises which might support them comfortably or even make them rich. But they were restricted to marriage with men of their own class and could only enter into a concubinage relationship with men of a higher class. In fact, the marital position of slaves and poor women was often entirely without legal sanction, even though their unions undoubtedly were recognized in their own circles. Poor and slave women were in a precarious situation. At times their only recourse was to register as prostitutes if they found themselves without conjugal or paternal support, or if they sought to be free of conjugal or paternal restraints.[18]

Occasionally, women of the highest ranks who were prepared to exchange respectability for freedom, registered as prostitutes to escape their familial restraints. Other women may have been removed forcibly from familial protection and forced into the marginal, anomalous population of women who legally had no fathers. It was the custom of most of the peoples of the Empire to expose babies whom they did not wish to raise. Often these infants died but contemporary observers noted that the healthy ones were often picked up to be raised and exploited as prostitutes.[19] Thus even many of the female babies who had been exposed by their parents did not die but entered into a life outside the boundaries of social respectability.

The ranks of these cast-offs must have been swollen by women who had been raised by their parents only to find themselves unable to secure a husband in adulthood. Often these women might enter into concubinage relationships with soldiers who, by law, were not allowed to marry during their term of service. Or they may have attempted to live without the support of men. The social structure simply provided no place for these women, and the old solution of ignoring their existence was becoming increasingly untenable in the turbulent world of the first century. Neither exposure, polygyny, nor even ordinary marriage seems to have worked to absorb women into the places allotted to them.

The complaints of male satirists which have survived the centuries provide us with just the smallest glimpses of women's devices for coping with the upheavals and insecurities of their world. One area in which women seem to have sought an outlet for their frustrations was surely religion. In the second century, Juvenal snarled that the all-woman cult of the Bona Dea, controlled by the matrons of Rome, had lost all respectability, serving only to mask orgies of unbridled lust.[20] Were his charges true or did they spring from the same fear of the unknown—in this case, gatherings of women without men—which gave rise to stories that the Christians indulged in cannibalistic orgies during their "love feasts?"[21]

The power of women in religion also disturbed Apuleius, whose strange novel, *The Golden Ass,* described the tribulations of a second-century hero who was turned into an ass as punishment for disturbing the rites of a coven of witches. It is unlikely that his readers took the story wholly as fantasy. Legislation against witchcraft, sorcery, sooth-saying, and charm-selling, activities which often provided a living for impoverished and lonely women, was reinforced by every emperor. Yet, increasingly wild accusations of witchcraft and poison, usually by women, troubled the entire imperial period.[22]

Apuleius' hero, Lucius, was finally saved through the beneficent power of Isis.[23] Ironically, she was a goddess whose worshippers in Hellenistic Egypt honored her because "she made the power of women equal to that of men."[24] As the great mother goddess, whose many names she took in her vision to Lucius, Isis had the power to reverse the witches' curse. In this aspect, she showed the other face of her *persona,* a love-goddess or whore whose worship was a sexual act. Her attraction for women may have been drawn from the same emotional sources as the popular early Christian romances, which centered upon the repentant whore with the heart of gold.

Eventually some similar tales would come to rest upon the character of Mary Magdalene, who appears in the New Testament not as a prostitute, but only as a woman possessed by demons who followed Jesus in gratitude for her exorcism.

Certainly, many Roman women must have been as revolted as the male satirists by the sexual license they found around them. Often, indeed, it was but a new form of tyranny for women.[25] Certainly poor women with no alternative to starvation except prostitution cannot have found much cause for celebration in the untrammeled sexual freedom of their age so admired by some modern writers.[26] For many women, the freedom to abstain from sexual activity must have appeared infinitely more desirable. Yet the validation of such a life of liberty would require the creation of a whole new social reality. At first, Isis was a leader in the field. Like the repentant whore, Thaïs of Alexandria, made famous in Christian legend, she became a champion of asceticism. The outraged Juvenal warned husbands against wives who "fill the house with covens of worshippers of strange oriental deities," who encourage them to torture and mutilate their bodies "to atone for having slept with their husbands the night before."[27]

The poet Propertius mocked the efforts of Augustus to revive the cults of Patrician and Plebeian chastity.[28] We should not be too quick to accept his mockery as proof that the cults lacked adherents among the women of Rome. As late as the seventh century, the site of the shrines was still known to Gregory I, and that great Christianizer of engrained pagan customs did not think it a waste of time to make it the assemblage point for consecrated widows who were to participate in the great religious processions of his pontificate.[29]

Similarly, Roman women continued to cling to the ideal of the *univira,* the woman who knew no man but her single husband, even though in practical fact the law prohibited widows from remaining unmarried if they were still of childbearing age. It was, therefore, always more a matter of sheer luck than of heroic fidelity that earned some women the title in their epitaphs.[30] As we noted earlier, angry mobs forced Augustus to recognize a longer period of widowhood for women than his marriage laws at first allowed. While some of the women of ancient Rome may well have enjoyed the sexual license that drew the attention of their male critics, others seem to have struggled to maintain themselves in chastity, both married and celibate, despite the systematic and inexorable pressures of custom strengthened by law and economic need.

The Emancipated Women of Christian Rome

The women of Rome were not subdued by the satirical poets who vented their anger against their freedom to live outside of male control. Some of them did no more than correct the grammar of their critical dinner partners. Others, as illustrated by repeated legislation against them, registered as prostitutes to secure their liberty from tutelage. Another group of emancipated women, gradually revealed in the Christian literature of the second century, sought liberty from sexual entanglements both within and outside of marriage. The weapons of social legislation and of satire failed to force these rebels into submission. Though they were declared abhorrent and untouchable, the anomalous woman persisted in troubling her critics.[31]

For some of these women, Christianity offered an avenue of escape from the insecurity of their marginal positions in the Roman world. Indeed, Christ may well have been among the "strange oriental deities" against whom Juvenal warned Roman husbands. But while the message of the Gospel was, as we have seen, a clear incitement to rebellion against the power of the family, the second generation of Christian men do not appear to have been as radical as Jesus. Paul himself condemned the impulse toward free love that apparently appeared among some of the Corinthians.[32] He reinforced Jesus' precept of monogamous, indissoluble marriage, which conformed to Roman principles if not to Roman practice.

As soon as it became clear that the second coming had been indefinitely postponed, the Fathers of the Church began to turn away from the extreme individualism of the first generation toward a more traditional order. During the last three decades of the first century, the loose Christian network began to solidify into a church. The New Testament was completed, though it would be another century before the canonical texts would be definitively set apart from the apocryphal gospels. The letters of Paul appear to have been revised and amplified. A handful of other texts by disciples of the second generation completed the fundamental apostolic corpus. With the possible exception of the *Epistle to the Hebrews,* the New Testament was wholly recorded by men.[33] The evangelists and the authors of the letters attributed to Paul, Peter, and others had the final word in shaping the Christian message. Women continued to contribute to the development of the new religion, but their writings, if they have been preserved at all, are concealed by anonymity. Beyond some chronicles that describe their activities, principally as martyrs, the lives and ideas of early Christian women can only be tentatively surmised by the use of highly indirect and perilously speculative methods.

The first of these is to try to imagine the appeal that the surviving Christian writings may have had for women. We do know for certain that the new religion was able to compete successfully with the cults of Bona Dea, Isis, and other pagan deities for the allegiance of Roman women. It must, therefore, have offered them advantages that they could not find in the "emancipated" life of Rome. It is, therefore, worthwhile to begin with a brief survey of the few texts remaining to us that record the earliest Christian views about the family relationships within which most women expected to pass their lives.

The Christians condemned all sexual relationships outside of marriage for men and women and expected men to keep their hearts as well as their bodies pure of lust. Thus Polycarp wrote to the community of Philippi, which had complained about a priest named Valens and deposed him for his covetous attitude toward the women of the congregation, that they were right not to tolerate his lust, though he urged that they treat the priest charitably if he could be brought to repent.[34] A visionary piece by Hermas that apparently occupied a prominent place in ancient liturgy, reiterated Jesus' prohibition against lust in the heart. In a vision, Mother Church rebuked the author for his unworthy thoughts at the sight of a woman named Rhoda, whom he saw bathing in the Tiber. She admonished him to keep his mind on his wife and not let it stray to any other woman.[35] Similarly, Ignatius warned the church at Antioch that husbands must love their wives, "remembering that, at the creation, one woman and not many was given to one man."[36]

An eloquent homily on conjugal chastity was attributed to Peter in a fictional account of his travels with his wife and companions:

> The chaste woman does not furnish occasions for being desired except by her husband. The chaste woman is grieved when she is desired by another. The chaste woman loves her husband from her heart, embraces, soothes, and pleases him, acts the slave to him, and is obedient to him in all things, except when it would be disobedient to God.[37]   .

Even in this traditional account of wifely love, therefore, "Peter" reinforced the message of Jesus that his followers must be prepared to leave anyone who interfered with their loyalty to him. Moreover, he stressed the equitable quality of Christian marriage as first delineated by Paul. The husband of a Christian wife must

> take his meals with her, keep company with her, go with her to the Word that makes chaste, not grieve her nor rashly quarrel with her, nor make himself hateful to her, furnishing her with all good things he can, and when he has them not, making up the deficiency with caresses.[38]

This sense of equality in marriage is a faint echo of the sentiment that "in Christ there is neither male nor female." However, the Christians of the second generation whose writings were deemed canonical by their successors rejected the transposition of this eschatalogical image to secular social relationships by persons who claimed that the "Resurrection" has occurred already. The Pastoral Letters attributed to Paul, added to the Canon before the end of the first century, reinforced the authority of the husband. The author of the second Epistle to Timothy warned against preachers who made their way into households and captivated "weak women, burdened with sin and swayed by various impulses, who will listen to anybody and can never arrive at knowledge of truth."[39]

Why did writers of this period feel so strongly that they must tell slaves to obey their masters, children to obey their parents, wives to obey their husbands? One would suppose that such commandments would hardly be needed in a world resting firmly on the twin pillars of paternal and patrician power. The widespread emancipation of Roman women from their ancient sexual and social subordination must have extended to Christian women, though it found different avenues of expression among them. Where pagan women may have taken lovers (though probably not in the numbers counted by their critics) and practiced contraception, Christian Roman women demanded that their husbands practice fidelity and refrain from exposing their infants. Still others may have left their husbands altogether, defied their parents by refusing marriage, or avoided maternity by refusing sexual relations. This tendency to independence alarmed the emerging Christian clergy as severely as it alarmed Juvenal and the imperial Roman legislators.

"Women shall be saved by bearing children," says one of the Pastorals.[40] The author of Colossians insisted on the preservation of the whole hierarchy of husbands, fathers, and masters.[41] In his visions, Mother Church threatened Hermas with punishment if he did not curb the unrestrained tongues of his wife and sons and promised that if he saved them he, too, would be saved.[42] When we remember that it was safer and more comfortable for women not to worship Christ in that age, we must wonder why they did not respond to such rebukes by transferring their allegiance to a friendlier deity. Perhaps Hermas' ''blasphemous'' wife and others like her were mollified by the moral restrictions Christianity placed on husbands. In an age of severely limited economic opportunities and unquestioned paternal control of children, many women may have found ample attraction in Christian prohibitions on divorce. The author of Ephesians likened the subjection of wife to husband to the subjection of the church to Christ but he also likened the love of husbands for wives to the love of Christ for the church.[43] Against the unyielding paternal power of the Roman father, I Timothy stressed the importance of the training and care that women give their children and encouraged them in love and piety and the fond expectation that their children would return these when age reversed their positions.[44] Parents were further cautioned to treat their children tenderly, to train them in godly ways, but to avoid provoking them to despair or anger.[45]

The treatment of adulterous wives, and the responsibilities of their husbands, were also modified. Hermas urged that men emulate Jesus and forgive their wives, separating from them only if they proved incorrigible.[46] If husbands took advantage of the crime to justify a divorce, they would have to live in continence as long as their wives survived.

In summary, while these writers tried to strengthen the traditional hierarchical family, they also sought to emphasize the reciprocal responsibilities of its members to one another and to soften the authority of the *pater familias* by subjecting him to sexual fidelity. The requirement that bishops approve and preside over the formation of Christian marriages, laid down by Ignatius, suggests that the infant church was already prepared to intervene in the marital difficulties of its members.[47] Moreover, some married women as well as some consecrated celibate women were able to extend the notion of partnership with men in a Christian life.

Several times, in the course of his visions, Mother Church told Hermas to hold his wife as a sister.[48] She simply may have meant to suggest that both marital partners were equal in the sight of God, a view that would conform to her warning that Hermas must avoid lust by turning to his wife. Considering the frequent use by later Christians of the brother-sister concept to describe couples who had forsworn their conjugal rights, it is possible that Hermas was preaching mutual continence within marriage. Alternatively, he merely may have been reinforcing the Pauline advice that Christians practice periodic abstinence to devote themselves to prayer.

There were, however, celibate Christians, and in the second century the evidence began to mount that their numbers were large. Those unmarried persons who were condemned as anomalous and unproductive in the laws of imperial Rome were viewed quite differently by early Christian leaders who saw them as intrinsic to their own emerging society. The unmarried required special attention from their ministers and a new set of moral precepts. For Christians, celibacy entailed sexual abstinence so complete that the two concepts tended almost to become synonymous. Far from seeing the asexual life as a barren exercise in self-indulgence, Christians followed Paul and the implicit example of Jesus in interpreting it as a divinely bestowed liberty which freed the practitioner for a fuller devotion. Thus Ignatius, who was destined to perish in the persecution of 110 AD, insisted that those who had the gift of remaining chaste outside of marriage must be allowed to do so. Indeed, he was the first of many moralists to criticize the chaste celibates for their pride and their tendency to boast that they were morally superior to the married bishops in authority over them.[49]

Among that proud company he counted widows as well as "those that are ever-virgin," both female and male:[50]

> Wives, be subject to your husbands and in the fear of God; and ye virgins to Christ in purity, not counting marriage an abomination, but desiring that which is better, not for the reproach of wedlock but for the sake of meditating on the law. . . . Husbands, love your wives as fellow servants of God, as your own bodies, as the partners of your lives and your co-adjutors in the procreation of children. Virgins, have Christ before your eyes, and His Father in your prayers, being enlightened by the spirit.[51]

Thus the vague approbation of the celibate course that we found in Paul is here reinforced by the acknowledgment that some people of both genders had taken an initiative not enjoined on them by Jesus or any of the apostles to renounce the sexual life completely. Ignatius, in fact, suggests that women in particular had to be counselled against adopting the virgin life out of hatred of marriage rather than the proper reason of religious devotion. Even the purest religious motivation, however, entailed a dramatic change in the definition of woman's purposes in life. The virgin life unequivocally entailed a mission beyond the sexual and procreative service of men. More-over, renunciation of marriage meant freedom from the subjection to husbands which Christian writers continued to insist was proper for wives.

The Ministry of Women

At the end of the first Christian century, a distinct clerical stratum was beginning to emerge. As the apostolic generation died out, the special distinction of the "twelve" was naturally diminished in favor of a broader group of bishops, priests, and deacons, who began to establish themselves as the directors of the congregations. Women, however, continued to share the work of prophecy where-by the faith was spread, just as they shared in the risks of martyr-dom. The limited information yielded by the sources for this period continues to support the idea that in other ways, too, Christianity of-fered devout women an active and fulfilling life capable of attracting pagan converts.

Prophecy was still an intrinsic part of the Christian mission and prophets generally were not brought into the emerging clerical hierarchy. They were itinerant preachers living for brief periods of time in the houses of the faithful and then moving on. In other cases, they were settled members of the community upon whom the Spirit chose to alight. Prophesying women are mentioned with apparent benevolence in the Pauline letter to the Corinthians. The Pastoral letters, however, give evidence of a spreading alarm over unli-censed prophets of both genders who were spreading "false doc-trines" of unspecified content.[52] The author of the *Book of Revela-tions,* addressed to the churches of Asia, similarly warned his readers against false prophets. He was particularly incensed against a woman of Thyatira, where Paul's convert, Lydia, had established the town's first congregation in her house. There, says the Rev-elator, "the woman Jezebel, who calls herself a prophetess, is teach-ing and beguiling servants to practice immorality and eat food sacri-ficed to idols."[53]

Among the teachers and prophets, who apparently occupied a

position parallel to, but not incorporated into, the clergy, were both female and male virgins. The first letter on virginity attributed to Clement of Rome warned male virgins against sharing their homes with maidens or even against eating with them:

> Others, again, meet together for vain and trifling conversation and merriment and that they may speak evil of one another; . . . Others gad about among the houses of virgin brethren or sisters on pretence of visiting them, or reading Scriptures or exorcising them. For as much as they are idle and do no work, they pry into things which ought not to be inquired into and, by means of plausible words, make merchandise of the name of Christ.[54]

Apparently, in larger cities, communities of consecrated virgins, clearly discernible to their neighbors, had already formed. These women and men kept company socially and joined in devotions of some sort together, exciting the hostility of the married clergy. A second letter on virginity, attributed to Clement, appears to have been addressed primarily to male virgins in the prophetic mission. It displays even greater urgency against the possibility of scandal and fatal seduction, cautioning unprotected men to avoid all contact with women whose freedom and vulnerability might prove too tempting:

> . . . with maidens we do not dwell, nor have we anything in common with them; with maidens we do not eat, nor drink; and where a maiden sleeps we do not sleep; neither do women wash our feet nor anoint us; and on no account do we sleep where a maiden sleeps who is unmarried or has taken the vow.[55]

Even where the virgin man was engaged in praying and preaching he should avoid the presence of women:

> But with us may no female, whether young maiden or married woman be there at that time; nor she that is aged, nor she that hath taken the vow; nor even a maid-servant, whether Christian or heathen; but there shall only be men with men. And, if we see it to be requisite to stand and pray for the sake of the women, and to speak words of exhortation and edification, we call together the brethren and all the holy sisters and maidens

and likewise all the other women who are there, inviting them with all modesty and becoming behavior to come and feast on the truth. . . . But the women and the maidens will wrap their hands in the garments; and we also, with circumspection and with all purity, our eyes looking upwards, shall wrap our right hand in our garments.[56]

Since the authorship and date of these letters are in dispute, we cannot use them securely for evidence on the exact regulations of the virginal life in the late first century. But they attest to an attitude that was certainly developing then and that continued to hold sway for the next century. While female virgins held a special place in the community, they were the objects of considerable fear and suspicion by the clergy, who could not look at them in their uncontrolled state without deep misgiving. The bishops, in particular, did not want them to join forces with virgin men to form a separate order of Christendom that might challenge their superiority and authority.

Among the scraps of memorabilia preserved by first-century Christians is a letter attributed to Ignatius of Antioch, addressed to the leading Christian widow of the age, the Virgin Mary herself. It congratulates her on her strong support of John in their joint struggle to establish the church in Asia. The author addresses her as "the lady of our new religion and repentance, handmaid among the faithful of all the works of piety."[57] Apocryphal as the letter probably is, it suggests that there were already Christians who advanced the mother of Jesus, whose active participation in the establishment of the church was held up for praise, as a model for widows and possibly for virgins too. At the same time, however, the patronizing tone of "Ignatius" suggests that he was anxious to assure episcopal control of these busy women.

The same author already had reason to worry about the influence of wealthy and influential women over the nascent episcopal community. A curious exchange of letters has been preserved, again tentatively attributed to Ignatius and a certain "Mary, the proselyte of Cassobelae," who enjoyed sufficient influence to nominate one of her protégés to a bishopric.[58] While women did not preside as bishops over Christian communities, they were nevertheless making bids to control the bishops themselves. Clearly, that power of manipulation through patronage was a form of indirect power that women of the first century sought to wield, just as their medieval counterparts would do later on.

This development inspired Ignatius to admonish his congregation at Philadelphia: "Let not the widows be wanderers about, nor fond of dainties, nor gadders from house to house; but let them be like Judith, noted for her seriousness; and like Anna, eminent for sobriety."[59] Similarly, the Pastoral Letters attributed to Paul stressed the need for modesty and for good deeds by women who profess religion.[60] Older women were directed not to be slanderous or drunk but to be reverent, sensible, domestic, chaste, kind, and submissive.[61] Who were these older women? Some of them may have been virgins, grown old in independent devotion. Others were probably clerical wives or widows consecrated to chastity.

Although women did not occupy the offices of deacon or bishop, the requirement that clerical wives be "serious, no slanderers, but temperate, faithful in all things," indicates that they were expected to take some supportive role in the care of the flock.[62] They probably took up many of the quasi-ministerial tasks often assigned to the wives of modern Protestant clergy. The *Didache,* which outlines some of the duties of the clergy and the order of services conducted at the end of the first century, indicates that a simple liturgy stressing communal prayers of thanksgiving, public confession of faults, and the commemorative sharing of bread and wine was still the general rule.[63] As long as these gatherings continued to take place in private homes, the wives of the clergy must have played some role in the administration and service of the meal, even if it were only the traditional role of hostess.

Such women, particularly the wives of bishops, must still have held important positions, particularly among the women of the community, after their husbands' deaths. Indeed, any prosperous Christian widow who had escaped tutelage by outliving her father or guardian or by acquiring the right of the three (or four) children, would have enjoyed all the legal and social freedom that distinguished her pagan counterparts. Their economic resources and social prestige must have guaranteed them a position of influence in the community even while it alerted a provident bishop to the dangers of their authority.

An obvious role for these women would have been the organization and administration of the care of widows and other indigent persons undertaken by every Christian community. We know that women certainly distinguished themselves in this service in later times, when evidence is more plentiful. This work did not require an apostolic mandate or sacramental powers, while it took full advantage of the women's capacities and resources. The assignment of this function to influential women may have off-set the attack on women's prophetic mission that began with the end of the first century. The forged correspondence between the Virgin Mary and Ignatius may have been intended to introduce the argument so prominent in succeeding centuries, that, in failing to make his mother one of the twelve apostles, Jesus condemned the evangelical mission of women.[64]

Clement of Rome, who died about 100, was one of the first to call for an end to women's ministerial functions. In an undisputed letter to the Corinthian community Clement rebuked wives who committed sedition against their husbands, reminding them of the fate of Lot's wife and other unfortunate biblical women.[65] The nature of the rebellion of the Corinthian wives is not clear, but Clement's solutions are. He ordered that services were to be conducted in a proper and settled manner, by appointed persons in the temple.[66] It is difficult to imagine Christians in this period having very many temples to accommodate this demand, but Clement was presenting a clear agenda. He wanted to see his congregations break away from the house churches with their informality and, probably, the equivocal presence of a forceful hostess. If services could be shifted to temples, the position of the clergy could be strengthened. His is the first firm declaration that a clergy has been based on apostolic succession and that "lay persons must be bound by the laws that pertain to the laity." Similarly, Polycarp of Smyrna commanded the youths and maidens of Philippi to be subject to deacons and presbyters as to God and Christ.[67] In brief, the faith was turning into a church; the church was organizing a clergy and relegating the laity to subordinate positions.

This deceptively simple division of the church into clergy and laity, however, created a potentially fatal asymmetry between women and men. In depriving religiously minded women of the opportunity to give full reign to their devotion, the clergy ran the risk of losing them altogether to competing religions which would welcome them warmly. Awareness of this problem may have caused the development of the tradition that Peter and the other Apostles had debated the question of a clerical ministry for women:

> Andrew said: Brothers it would be useful to assign a ministry to women. Peter said: Then let us so order it; we might make known to them the accurate offering of the body and blood.

John said: Brothers, you are forgetting that the Master, when he would pray with bread and cup and bless them, saying This is my body; This is my blood; did not permit them to stand with us. Martha said: Because of Mary, because he saw her laughing. Mary said: I laugh no more: for he said to us then that the weak would be saved by the strong. Cephas said: You must also remember that women cannot stand up to pray but must sit on the ground. James said: Therefore in what way can we decree a ministry for women except a diaconate which serves needy women?[68]

An obvious role for the deaconesses, whose existence in this period is attested in all the available sources, was to mediate between the widows and virgins who lived outside of the control of husbands and the clergy, who were wary of coming too close to them. Deaconesses were given the responsibility for instructing female catechumens and even baptizing them, a sacramental role they would lose in later centuries.[69] The Pastoral Letters command that they be serious, temperate, and faithful.[70] The Letters expressly forbade the deaconesses to instruct men, on the grounds that Adam took precedence in the order of creation, but Eve in the order of sin.[71] Instead the Letters envisaged deaconesses as the instructors of younger women and admonished them to teach those women good doctrine and to love their husbands and children.[72] In Hermas' vision, Mother Church directed him to make copies of her teachings, including her admonitions against his talkative wife, and send a copy to Clement (perhaps to support him against the seditious women of Corinth) and to Grapte, probably a deaconess, "who will admonish the widows and orphans."[73]

The second century began, therefore, with a distinct trend in the church toward the segregation of women, not only from the clergy but from the male laity as well; in some areas, churches were constructed with separate galleries for women. Deaconesses appear to have conducted their activities in their households. Since their mission was to widows and orphans, persons who were not under the control of husbands and fathers, the deaconesses may have become the center of the community of consecrated women.

No source gives directions regarding the marital status of these deaconesses. They may have been married women, perhaps the wives of priests and deacons. In that case, the clergy may have envisaged that they would draw their authority from that of their husbands and that they could be counted on to instruct their charges as they themselves were instructed. But husbands die and the indications are that in that period they often died before their wives, so that women who may have begun the diaconate as married women must have ended as consecrated widows.

The ''order'' of widows as Paul conceived it had no special duties except prayer. Its relationship to the female diaconate was never clarified, though it does seem clear, given their responsibilities, that deaconesses must have been consecrated before the canonical age of sixty, which distinguished widows. Peter was said to have instituted three orders of widows: two devoted to prayer for the rest of the faithful and the transmission of those revelations which customarily come to the contemplative; a third to sit with women in danger of death, to do good works selflessly and soberly, and to keep vigil with other women in the night. Particularly, they were to act as go-betweens, relaying the needs of the indigent and invalid to presbyters and deacons and returning with the necessary help.[74] As a community of consecrated virgins began to emerge, they, too, were probably associated with these good works. None of the sources say so but, again, to judge from later evidence, the early clergy must soon have determined that it was necessary to put young unmarried women under some sort of supervision and the widows and deaconesses were the logical candidates for the job.

In short, the Christians confronted the stress arising out of the presence of growing numbers of celibate women in Roman society by revising the structure that excluded them. The creation of an ''order'' of widows and virgins under the ministry of a female diaconate was an original and successful solution to the problem of the unplaced woman. At worst, it represented a fictive family, loosely tied to the clerical hierarchy which could exercise some form of paternalistic supervision. At best, it turned the unmarried woman's autonomy into a positive asset by creating new social roles for her to play. In either case, however, the trend toward confining the mission of women to other women was a source of new stress. The lines of authority passing from bishops through priests and deacons to laymen, and from laymen to their wives and children, still bypassed consecrated women, their deaconesses, and the prophetic community.

FIGURE 4. Orant with group of men. Rome sarcophagus detail. From Grabar, André, *Early Christian Art* (New York: Odyssey Press, 1968), plate 269.

Chapter Four:
Your Daughters Shall Prophesy

The decisions to provide the church with an established clerical hierarchy and to return to traditional family morality were rooted in the recognition that Jesus' second coming had been delayed and a future of unforeseeable length lay before the human race. Not all Christians, however, accepted these modifications. Many continued to pursue the radical social changes implicit in the evangelical message. From them, the ideal of virginity as the fullest formulation of the Christian life emerged and, with it, a group of women who tore themselves loose from the old social fabric to devise a new way of life. Their rejection of husbands, homes, and children was a genuine revolution, which they accomplished despite the preference of the Christian fathers of this period for a more traditional social morality.

The women of the Roman Empire had a hundred cults from which to choose. Christianity was one choice, but Christians were generally despised. The majority lacked social status and they were regularly accused of atheism at best and cannibalism at worst. Moreover, a constant threat of lynching dogged Christian prophets and their followers.[1] On the other hand, many other cults offered greater social prominence and a strong leadership role to women. The women of the Roman Empire could have chosen to worship female deities or to embrace such rarefied philosophical sects as the neo-Pythagoreans.[2] Their choice of Christianity would be quite inexplicable if second-century women saw its leaders as misogynistic defenders of the subordination of their sex.

Quite the contrary, Christianity was widely viewed and scorned by educated pagans as a religion of women and slaves. The anti-Christian Celsus maintained that the proponents of the faith increased their numbers by infiltrating houses and seducing women and children.[3] On the other side, some of the greatest women in the

Empire showed an interest in the faith, culminating at the end of the second century with the invitation of the Empress Julia Mammaea to Origen to expound its principles to her.[4] Though we have only the scantiest information concerning individual converts during the centuries of persecution, there is a repeated theme in early Christian literature, borne out by the more concrete traditions of martyrdom, that suggests that the majority of upper-class Christians were women.

This demographic peculiarity clearly reflects the condition of these women in Roman society. The public lives of men required regular participation in the liturgies of stata paganism. Men of the ruling classes who became Christian would have to sacrifice their careers and much of their social lives in order to avoid these ceremonies. In addition, they were in constant danger of denunciation to a persecuting authority or the unpredictable violence of an angry mob. Ironically, women, barred as they were from public life, were always in less danger of discovery, except from members of their immediate family circle.[5] Moreover, resentment over their exclusion from public life may have heightened the attraction of a faith that denigrated the importance of worldly offices and powers.

The faith they espoused, moreover, may have been a more direct outgrowth of the radical message of the gospels than the writings of the Christian Fathers seem to indicate. Early Christian communities were open to many ideas less orthodox or less traditional in nature. The authority of the clergy was still very much in a formative stage and its network was far from complete. Christianity was still subject to influences from other schools of thought and from the individual visions of charismatic prophets, who were often able to attract followers who maintained their teachings for generations after their deaths.[6]

In some communities and in innumerable households where women lived isolated from the world, the teaching ministry was carried on wholly without benefit of clergy. Unstructured groups, under the presidency of teachers of both genders, still gathered excitedly to discuss the implications of the new ideas. Only late in the second century did the episcopate begin to isolate, criticize, and condemn theological deviants and lay out the lines of a strict orthodox teaching.[7] At that time they were confronted with a variety of ideas loosely characterized as "gnostic," whose preachers were said to be possessed of secret, revealed knowledge.

The Heterodox Teaching of Christian Women

Central to the ideas of the gnostic teachers were a series of questions regarding the relationship of spirit and flesh, of mind and matter. This problem had preoccupied religious and philosophical
theorists for many centuries before Jesus was born. As Christians
began to compete for the minds and hearts of the people of the
Graeco-Roman world, they could not avoid its challenge. The
gnostic concept of a descending hierarchy, from the height of
perfect spirit to the depths of inert matter, had obvious similarities to
Christianity's faith in the ultimate salvation of the soul. The attraction of the spiritual life could not help but suggest rejection of the
flesh and the social life built up in the world upon the need to
reproduce the flesh. However, there were intellectual and social
consequences to be drawn from the gnostic ideal that were inherent-
ly inimical to the basic principles of the new religion.

About the middle of the second century, Irenaeus, Bishop of
Lyon, undertook to write a massive book systematically defending
orthodox Christianity as taught by the Christian clergy. He had been
moved to do so because of the increase in heterodox sects in Gaul.
He testified that groups of women from every walk of life were
leaving homes, parents, and husbands to follow prophetic teachers
of dubious character. In his own Rhône Valley, Irenaeus had
firsthand knowledge of a prophet named Marcus, who had gained
inordinate influence among the women of his congregations. According to Irenaeus, he converted them to his flock by seducing
them sexually, using love potions on women who resisted his blan-
dishments. He accused him of using his prophetic gifts to bilk
women of their property in exchange for a share of his prophetic
power. These women prophesied during the meetings of his
followers, and also participated with him in liturgies involving a
consecrated chalice.[8]

Irenaeus further claimed that other women left their husbands to
follow certain gnostic prophets who promised that they would live
as brother and sister while spreading the gospel together. Irenaeus
put no credence in such promises. He thought that the demands of
the flesh would overcome even the best intentions. Moreover, like
the author of the Clementine "Letters on Virginity," he was concerned about the reputations of orthodox preachers if such hypo-
critical associations became too general. Second-century tongues

were as prone to gossip as our own, and pagans were not over-scrupulous in distinguishing orthodox from heterodox Christians.

In our own time, we have surely seen too many contemporary ex-amples of the sexual exploitation of women by self-appointed cult leaders not to agree that Irenaeus had a point. Nevertheless, we should grant that some of these heterodox couples probably were in-nocent of all sexual contact. Everything that we have already con-jectured about the milieu of women attracted to Christianity points to a widespread impulse to free themselves from the bonds and obligations of marriage without falling into the prostitution that was its usual complement. Moreover, gnostic preachers, and some or-thodox ones as well, genuinely sought to discover a way of life that transcended the demands of the flesh. In the second century, this was widely expressed in the popularity of a romance called *The Acts of Paul and Thecla,* which concerned the heroic adventures of a young woman who abandoned home, family, and fiancé to practice the life of virginity as she heard Paul preach it. The culmination of the story is Thecla's fierce defense of her faith and her way of life in the face of imperial persecution and her dramatic self-baptism in the arena as the beasts are about to be loosed upon her.[9]

Irenaeus' attack on the heretics involved certain assumptions about the Christian cosmos which must have been current among the clergy, though they had not yet been clearly delineated by theo-logians. His definitions of the doctrines of the faith were uncompro-misingly monotheistic, excluding from the chain between God and man the entire Platonic progression of divine and semi-divine beings whom the gnostics had added.[10] His God was unique, set apart from all his creatures and, though a trinity, entirely male in nature. Some of the gnostics, on the other hand, suggested that at least one major member of the trinity might be a mother.[11]

Irenaeus denied any suggestion that Christ, though God, was in any sense not a full human being from the moment of his conception until his ascent into heaven. This refuted dualists, like the popular prophet Marcion, who represented Jesus as the spirit of good op-posed to the spirit of evil represented by the God of the Old Testa-ment, and the docetics, who taught that Jesus was a pure spirit only, and the illusion of his birth and sufferings had been concocted by the devil to mislead us as to the nature of human flesh.

Why should women have been attracted to these gnostic sects, as they certainly appear to have been? It is unlikely that the occasional suggestion that God has a partially female nature can explain the phenomenon. The idea was, after all, not new to the classical world; the cults of the various powerful goddesses of the Hellenistic world must have had much more to offer in that respect than the very faint female component of the gnostic pantheon. It is possible, however, that some women who were attracted to the Christian message (or some variant thereof) turned to gnostic prophets because they were repelled by the misogyny of some of the clerical representatives of orthodox Christianity.

It is very difficult to be persuaded that the gnostics offered women a more favorable view of their gender than did the orthodox. The docetics, who denied the humanity of Jesus, were unable to find any redeeming virtue in the participation of his human mother in his great work. The cosmic visions of Valentinian and others, who combined some elements of the Jewish tradition of creation with the fall of the neo-Platonic hierarchy, did not differ from the orthodox in blaming women for the fall of man. Though there were many variations, one basic story emerged from their teachings: the impertinent, or deluded Aeon-mother, Sophia, was entangled by her pride or weakness into carnal desires. As a result, she gave birth to lower forms of beings and ultimately fell into the trap of matter which now holds fast the human spirit. Because of that female impulse to procreate, because of that fatal lustfulness, the flesh that imprisons us came into being.

The *Exegesis of the Soul,* an Egyptian tract of about 200 AD, depicted the soul as a female virgin fallen into the clutches of one heartless seducer after another; ever abandoned, ever obliged to seek a new protestor, until at last she is abandoned and starving.[12] Similarly, the father of all the heretics, Simon Magus, was said to have claimed that in his companion Helen, the prostitute, he had seen and rescued the very Aeon whose humiliation had caused the fall.[13] The Encratites, whose asceticism enticed the Christian apologist, Tatian, into heresy taught that woman was a creation of the devil, as was the lower half of man.[14]

Perhaps their female listeners were less concerned with the cause of our mortal dilemma than with the proposed cure. All the gnostic teachers seem to have shared a conviction that the illumination of knowledge which they shared with their followers elevated them to an elite circle of the spiritually perfect, regardless of gender. In this sense, gnosticism offered to women and to lay men an alternate hierarchy to that of the clergy. It is also probably true, as their critics charged, that some gnostic circles did claim freedom from the sexual restraints that sin had laid on the ignorant. Some women must have found the notion of "free love" divorced from the family hierarchy appealing.

Other groups, like the Encratites, saw procreation as the diabolically inspired evil that perpetuates our imprisonment within these mortal coils.[15] They argued that total purity would disentangle trapped souls, reuniting them with the light. Other gnostic texts argued that the resurrection would bring the abolition of the procreative works of women.[16] Every sexual act being an act of adultery, true marriages would join only the souls of the partners.[17] Indeed, "the partners of the spiritual marriage do not weary and abandon one another for they become one flesh and the soul is joined to her true master."[18] Where else should those women have looked, who still sought a world in which there would be neither male nor female?

There does not seem to have been a great deal of difference between the preaching of heterodox and orthodox men on the question of the unsavory qualities of women and their culpability for the curse of the flesh. However, we have only a small portion of gnostic literature, preserved by chance in out-of-the-way places or in the works of critics. We cannot, therefore, assume that the old allegorical identification of woman and flesh, man and spirit, was always accepted by women. There were female preachers among the gnostics, as we have seen, and they may have used quite a different set of metaphors. The extant works of male ascetics combine revulsion from the flesh with revulsion from women. Their pagan contemporaries were similarly prone to fantasies in which female witches changed them into animals in the course of sexual intercourse.[19] Female preachers and their female audiences, while still accepting the gnostic message concerning the inherent evil of the flesh, may have experienced a similar revulsion and felt those fears in quite a different manner.

When we consider again that this was a world in which women were brought to their marriage beds by parents or guardians whose power was reinforced by a paternalistic state, we must concede the possibility that sexuality itself became revolting to many women. If fastidious males were disgusted by the physical facts of sex and childbirth, it would have been very strange if women had not shuddered at least as violently at the thought of a procreative process over which they had no control. Even in the best of circumstances, not every woman takes naturally to maternity. Where her wishes about pregnancy were discounted and her husband had the un-contested legal power to decree whether or not the ensuing baby would live, the most maternal of women might draw back.

In the second century, life for many women entailed enforced vir-tue or enforced vice. When they heard a prophet preach that the flesh was evil, their own experience could testify that it was so. When they saw a mystical route to escape from the flesh, it is no wonder that they took it. Even when the message itself was rooted deeply in misogynistic premises, individual women may have wondered how they had become victims of their fragile bodies if they had not somehow incurred a penalty for some obscure and dis-tant wrong-doing. Other women may have believed that their own acceptance of the preachers' message liberated them from the fe-male fate and therefore exempted them from female disabilities.

When a woman preached, who can say what vistas may have opened to her sisters? We have already noted that Marcus in Lyon shared the ritual of consecrating the cup of prophecy with a woman; in the early third century, the doctrines of Marcion were prom-ulgated by a prophetess named Philumene.[20] The Collrydians were women who assembled and performed priestly functions at services in honor of the Virgin Mary.[21] In brief, one attraction—and a powerful one—that the heterodox alternatives to the church offered to women was an active clerical and teaching role. Another was the opportunity to cast off the constraints of marriage and childbirth, an idea spread by women prophets to distant parts of the Empire. The struggle between the prophets and the priests intensified toward the end of the second century.[22]

It was Tertullian who launched a generalized attack on the female ministry. He said that a woman named Marcellina was the propo-nent of Marcionism in Rome and that she said her teaching was based on personal revelations from Mary, Salome and Martha: "These heretic women! How shameless! They dare to teach, to argue, to act as exorcists, to promise healing in return and even, perhaps to baptize."[23] Indeed Tertullian was in advance of general church practice in the condemnation of all baptism by women and his attack on the legendary self-baptism of Thecla:

> Oh, the wantoness of a woman who dares to teach. At least, let her not give birth to the right of baptising unless that new beast should come forth that whoever would obtain baptism should confer it on themselves. Some maintain that Paul, through the

example of Thecla, gave women license to teach and baptize; they knew a priest in Asia who construes that scripture as the fulfillment of Paul, proving and acknowledging her to have acted for love of Paul, to have gone away from that place. How can this be seen as the faith—that is, the teaching and baptising of women who never permitted it to women? Let them be silent, he said, and ask their husbands at home.[24]

Who was the priest of Asia? Very probably it was Montanus, whose preachings were transmitted to Tertullian's province of Africa by prophetesses, who were destined to draw the mighty misogynist himself into heresy. Phrygia, the home of the cult of the Great Mother, was a popular source of prophetesses at this period. In Thyatira, where Lydia had established a church in Paul's time, "Jezebel" had led a community rivalling that of the author of the *Apocalypse* and where Montanism later flourished was in that province. Bithynia, where Pliny found a church led by deaconesses, was not far away. Firmillian described the attempts of one prophetess from nearby Cappadocia to lead her followers to Jerusalem.[25] In Asia Minor, then, there were women who did not accept the ban on prophesy without rebuttal. There the graves of Philip's four prophetic daughters were still held in honor.

Montanus himself may have been a priest of Cybèle before his conversion to Christianity.[26] He began his preaching in Phrygia about 172 AD, emphasizing an ascetic doctrine spread by two prophetesses, Priscilla and Maximilla. A hundred years later, Eusebius remembered them and their revolt against episcopal power in favor of the ecstatic power of prophesy, for even in the age of Constantine their tradition had not died. Maximilla was proclaimed The Paraclete by her followers before she died in 179.[27] Eusebius recalled that when Bishop Serapion of Antioch tried to exorcise her of the spirit, she resisted, crying out: "I am driven as a wolf from the sheepfold. But I am not a wolf! I am the word, the spirit and the power!"[28]

The teachings of Priscilla and Maximilla have been preserved only by their enemies and their famous disciple Tertullian who, of course, spoke with his own voice at all times. Certainly they supported the principle of prophetic revelation against that of episcopal authority and, at least by implication, the prophetic ministry of women. Their ideas seem to have been fuelled by a renewed sense that time was growing short. Perhaps the outbreak of widespread persecution under Marcus Aurelius revived the expectation of the imminent second coming of Jesus. Tertullian noted that growing numbers of women in his province of Africa embraced a life of sexual abstinence and refused to contribute to the continuation of the material world by their participation in the process of procreation.[29] His own deep distrust of that commitment to the world led him to launch the full-scale attack on second marriages (which he called "digamy"), which finally resulted in his breach from the orthodox church.[30]

The teachings of the Montanists were no mere passing phenomena. A hundred years later Eusebius said that Christians were still trying to refute Maximilla's prophesies on the grounds that they had not come true. Eusebius still thought it worthwhile to discredit Priscilla's claim to virginity by charging that she and Maximilla had deserted their husbands.[31] (We have lost the content of the prophesies themselves, so we do not know upon what grounds they based their claims to virginity.) The worst that Hippolytus could allege against them in his book against heresy was that their followers "introduced novelties of fasts and feasts, meals of parched food and repasts of radishes, alleging that they had been so instructed by the women."[32] In these Montanist communities, under the presidency of prophetesses, we can clearly discern the antecedents of those ascetic communities which would begin to flourish in the Egyptian deserts a hundred years later.

The Orthodox Preaching of Women

Among the orthodox, too, itinerant preachers moving from town to town still provided a source of doctrine independent of the settled clergy, who were still not numerous enough or strong enough to affect every Christian household. "Clement of Rome" had spoken, with some distaste, of informal local meetings for joint prayers, discussions, and exorcisms as characteristic of the religious customs of the virginal communities.[33]

In the previous chapter, we noted that "Clement" was anxious to keep male virgins from serving communities where the only Christians were women. But if communities of women could not take advantage of the chance presence of a wandering preacher, they would have no access to any kind of clerical ministry since, clearly, there were no bishops or priests among their number. "Clement" asserted that his intention was not to denigrate his Christian sisters but only to protect his brothers from temptation.[34] Apparently he thought that women could carry on adequate religious lives without the help of the clergy.

How would these communities made up only of women have functioned? I have already argued that women were active evangelists. Their impact would clearly have been strongest within their own *familiae*, particularly in those sections of the Roman Empire where it was customary to confine female members of the household to their own quarters and forbid them the freedom of the public streets. The transcript of the trial, in the middle of the second century, of Justin Martyr and his companions, one of whom was a woman, indicates that several of these martyrs had received their faith from their parents.[35] It is highly probable that women then, just as in better documented later periods, led this domestic mission, carrying their religion with their trousseaux into new households.[36]

Despite the ideals of Clement of Rome and his contemporaries, most Christian congregations did not have temples and did not enjoy the services of a settled clergy.[37] In house churches, the natural presidency of the hostess would still have a powerful effect. Although an emerging sacramental quality to the worship is apparent in the *Didascalia,* the testimony of Justin Martyr suggests a far more informal norm for the mid-second century. He described simple meetings of the faithful to hear inspirational addresses followed by a shared meal of bread and wine in memory of Jesus.[38] Pliny described a similar, simple ceremony in his report to Hadrian, based on the testimony of two deaconesses.[39]

Justin indicated that the distribution of the bread and wine was not assigned to bishops or priests, but to deacons.[40] Though he made no mention of deaconesses in this connection, it seems likely that they must have performed this service for communities without deacons. We know that they undertook the other important sacramental service of baptism for women, since it was considered unfitting for the male clergy to have such close contact with female catechumens.[41] Where it was the practice to reserve portions of the bread and wine for absent members of the community, deaconesses probably administered this communion to women who were sick or unable to leave their houses. Certainly, it was to deaconesses that Pliny was directed when he wished to investigate the Christians of Bithynia, in Asia Minor.[42]

We are on firmer ground in conjecturing that orthodox women prophesied and generally taught in communities where there were no male clergy, and even, perhaps, where there were. Even the author of the pseudo-Clementine homilies, which purported to record Peter's teaching, gave grudging recognition to female prophecy despite his inclination toward a gnostic rejection of the female gender:

> Let them understand that there are two kinds of prophecy: the one female, the other male; and let it be divined that the first, being the male, has been ranked before the other in the order of advent; but the second being female, has been appointed to come first in the order of pairs.[43]

> This second, therefore, being amongst those born of women as the female superintendent of this present world, wishes to be thought masculine. Wherefore, stealing the seeds of the male and sowing them with her own seeds of flesh, she brings forth fruits, that is words, as wholly her own.[44]

Thus, even though it was often regarded as an insolent assumption of masculine authority, the preaching of women was recognized as a legitimate form of prophecy. Therefore, if some men wanted to control worship in the churches and segregate themselves from partnership with women in the Christian life, many women may have been satisfied to let them go their way, preferring to carry on their real religious life within their own communities.

In short, the tendency of the early church to exclude and silence women may have been less apparent in the second century than it is now. The clergy's ultimate goal of superiority may have been obscured by the increasing segregation that resulted from their misogyny.[45] Influential and wealthy women probably never were silenced, even if they wished to speak in church, even before a bishop. But the active and genuinely interesting aspects of their religious lives were probably expressed in a more private ministry.

To begin with, all Christians had a mission to teach by example, not only through the drama of martyrdom but also in the conduct of daily life. The mistress who treated her slaves with respect for their common humanity; the slave whose dignity under humiliating circumstances or heroism in rejecting the vices of owners defied the normal rules of self-interest; the widow who shared her small portion with those more needy than herself; the sister or neighbor ready with comfort in time of trouble, were all familiar and exemplary types of female Christianity.

More directly, the charismatic appeal of individual women made them eloquent exponents of the teachings of Jesus. Tatian and Clement of Alexandria both observed that women taught by word as well as example among the Christians of the second century.[46] In his "Address to the Greeks," Tatian eloquently defended the respect that Christians commonly paid to their female teachers, suggesting that their mission was not confined to women alone:

> . . . you should not regard as something strange what you find among us, for compared with the (pagan) statues (of famous women) which are before your eyes, you should not treat with scorn the women among us who pursue philosophy. Your Sappho is a lewd, lovesick female singing her own wantonness; but all our women are chaste, and the maidens at their distaffs sing of divine things more nobly than that damsel of yours. Wherefore, be ashamed, you who are professed disciples of women, to scoff at those of the sex who hold our doctrine, as well as at the solemn assemblies which they frequent.[47]

In the Roman world of the second century, women were present at banquets and other public events and did not fear to voice their opinions in mixed company. There is no reason to imagine that Christian women were backward in pressing their beliefs in similar circumstances. However, as time passed, Christians came to distrust uncontrolled prophecy, and the unlicensed teacher. At the end of the second century, Tertullian drew an intriguing picture of the position of a prophetess in an orthodox community:

> We have now among us a sister whose lot it has been to be favored with sundry gifts of revelation, which she experiences in the Spirit by ecstatic vision amidst the sacred rites of the Lord's Day in the church: she converses with angels and sometimes even with the Lord; she both sees and hears mysterious communications; some men's hearts she understands and to them who are in need she distributes remedies. Whether it be in the reading of the scriptures, or in the changing of psalms, or in the preaching of sermons, or in the offering up of prayers, in all those religious services, matter and opportunity are afforded to her of seeing visions. It may possibly have happened to us, whilse this sister of ours was rapt in the Spirit, that we had discourses in some ineffable way

about the soul! After the people are dismissed at the conclusion of the sacred services, she is in the regular habit of reporting to us whatever things she may have seen in vision (for all her communications are examined with the most scrupulous care, in order that the truth may be probed).[48]

The clergy of the community may have excluded women from the performance of the services, but this woman clearly excluded them from her most important religious experiences. In the middle of the second century, according to Justin Martyr, Christian women were still recognized as orthodox preachers.[49] By the century's end, Tertullian seems to present us with a strange competition between the clerical liturgy and the private revelations of a female prophet transmitted in the church on Sundays. By the middle of the third century, Cyprian, bishop of Carthage, referred to women participating in orthodox services as a thing of the past.[50]

In brief, the period when women followed heterodox preachers and women prophets were forming their own congregations was also a period of marked decline in female orthodox preaching.[51] But before they disappeared from the scene, these preachers had formulated and transmitted a vital and revolutionary social message to the growing Christian community. In part, they derived it from the gnostic rejection of the flesh. Tatian, their champion, ended his life as an Encratite, arguing that the flesh was evil and could be overcome only by complete sexual purity. There was also, however, a movement among women, expressed in preaching and writing, that remained orthodox theologically, while forcing open the barriers of the social structure against the autonomous women who lived beyond the roles imposed by gender.

The Flight from Sexuality

What was the content of their teaching? They must have drawn most of it directly from the scriptures, as male preachers did. In addition, they had access to another body of material which seems more closely designed to appeal to the interests of women—the apocryphal gospels.[52] These works probably originated in the second and early third centuries in Christian communities of Syria and Egypt, where evidence is strongest for the segregation of women, and where a tendency to asceticism was evident long before the dramatic growth of desert monasteries in the fourth century.[53]

Modern students of these works have generally abandoned the idea that they represent early Christian forgeries competing with the standard corpus of the New Testament for inclusion in the Christian Bible. They are now generally viewed as a species of didactic novels or romances, not unlike fictional works of an uplifting nature that have been consistently employed in the service of Christian piety ever since.[54]

The apocryphal books often feature characters from the Gospels and are sometimes written in the first person. Neither device was outside the novelistic traditions of the age. Seen in this light, there is growing agreement that the apocrypha qualify as legitimate and valuable documents for the study of the obscure religious life of the second-century Christian communities. Their lively stories and exotic settings provide a pleasant framework for more serious preaching. They were ideally fashioned to appeal to an audience of women—the novel-reading public of the Hellenistic world. Indeed, like many novels ever since, it is very likely that many of them were written by women.[55]

The *Acts* of John, Peter, Paul, Andrew, Thomas, and Xantippe present material centered on female characters and female interests. Not only do they lack the misogyny that was beginning to show itself in so many patristic productions of this period, but they exhibit a generalized hostility to men in depicting the struggles of heroic women to free themselves from paternal or conjugal demands. Sometimes they convey an air of faint disappointment or disapproval of their male mentors who are insufficiently supportive in the struggle. The emphasis on female characters and, indeed, the very anonymity of the works, argue that the authors were women who, sensitive to the prejudices of both Christian and Pagan audiences, sought cover for their ideas. To be sure anonymous is still anonymous. No certain identification of these authors can be made at this late date. But there is a case for presumption in favor of female origin. Furthermore, it is not difficult to imagine that the communities of Christian women largely separated from the influence of the nascent clergy, generated a body of material which emphasized areas of social theology not discussed in patristic sources of the period. These ideas may have been spread among the communities by wandering male preachers sympathetic to women's concerns, by women devoted to the evangelistic mission, or by other women travelling more conventionally from one household to another.

The apocryphal gospels concern the fictional adventures of

biblical characters after the Resurrection. The *Acts* that probably came from the female communities emphasize the roles of female devotees. Some of these are women mentioned in the New Testament whose later lives and adventures were of obvious interest to their successors. The *Acts of Bartholomew,* for example, include tales of Mary Magdalene, Salome, Mary and Martha of Bethany, and the woman whose sins were forgiven. Joanna renounces her husband's bed as a result of her conversion. Leah (the widow from Nain) and "Berenice," the hemorraging woman, are given active roles in the prophetic mission.[56] The latter, as "Veronica," appeared in the *Acts of Pilate* trying to enter the court to defend Jesus. She was driven back by the contemptuous judges, who refused to admit the testimony of women.[57]

Towering above this female company of apostles is the Virgin Mary, the mother of Jesus. Her importance in Christian worship clearly appears to have grown out of the communities that produced the apocrypha. As we have seen, Mary did not play a very prominent role in the New Testament except as a symbol of the newly emerging people of God, a second Eve, a type of Mother Church, and the first member of Jesus' eschatological family. Neither *The Acts of the Apostles* nor the assorted apostolic letters incorporated into the New Testament provide a clue to her activities in the infant church after Pentecost. The authors and readers of the apocryphal gospels, however, maintained a lively interest in her later career and the principal elements of her cult were formulated there. These texts introduced elements that went far beyond the evangelical accounts, and were introduced into patristic writings only a century or so later. If, therefore, I am correct in arguing that the apocryphal gospels reflect the ideas of consecrated women of the second and early third centuries, then these women were the developers of the cult of Mary, which was only later incorporated into orthodox dogma.[58]

The doctrine of the immaculate conception of Mary, which was only endorsed by the Catholic Church in modern times, was fully formulated in the *Protoevangelion of James,* a book attributed to the brother of Jesus. Following certain tried and true biblical precedents, the author conjectured that Mary's mother, Anna, was a barren wife, tormented and persecuted by malicious women in that fertility-centered age. Her husband, believing that the misfortune arose from some misdeed on his part, went into the desert to repent, leaving Anna to mourn him as dead. Happily, an angel heard her

wailing and impregnated her by supernatural means. Her husband
returned. Together they rejoiced in the birth of their daughter,
Mary.[59] The story goes on to tell of Mary's childhood, her upbring-
ing in the Temple with the aid of angels, and her other-worldly purity. She entered the world outside for the first time when the onset of
menstruation threatened to pollute the sacred premises as the betrothed of Joseph, who had been specially picked from several candidates as the husband most likely to preserve her virginity.[60]

The doctrine of the perpetual virginity of Mary was put forward
in the same book. The author, writing in the first person as the apostle James, brother of Jesus, maintained that his brothers and sisters
were Joseph's children by an earlier marriage (a notion wholly un-
supported by the New Testament). Mary is drawn as a fond and
careful stepmother.[61] The narrative further proclaims that she retained her virginity even after the birth of Jesus. A woman named
Salome (who is not specifically identified as the woman at the foot
of the cross) is introduced as a midwife who performed a physical
examination of the new mother and testified that she had remained
miraculously intact.[62] A more discreet version was advanced in the
Gospel of Bartholomew, in which Mary's attempt to verbalize the
mystery of Jesus' birth created a physical upheaval that threatened
to destroy the world.[63]

The Gospel of Bartholomew depicted Mary as an active disciple,
engaging in arguments with the other apostles on various points and
instructing them on the events of Jesus' early life. The author even
placed her in the traditional position of Mary Magdalene as the first
witness to the resurrection, emphasizing that the male apostles were
in hiding at the time.[64] A group of texts emanating principally from
Egypt preserved a variety of traditions concerning Mary's later life.
They picture her living in Ephesus with Salome, Joanna, and some
of her girlhood companions from the Temple, where they turned the
house of John into an evangelical center devoted to the spreading of
Jesus' message.[65] The same texts maintained that Mary habitually
received visits from the other apostles and served as a guide to them,
a font of doctrine, and finally a genuine cult figure in her own right.
Evodius, Bishop of Antioch, was the first to claim that he had heard
of her assumption from an eyewitness.[66] The doctrine was
elaborated in the Egyptian apocrypha which described the death of
Mary. Surrounded by the apostles, she delivered her last remon-
strances and then, in accordance with a promise given by Jesus, was
carried bodily, and still incorruptible, into heaven by a band of
angels.[67]

With Mary as an exemplary cult figure, the women of the second century began to enunciate a more detailed doctrine of virginity as the life of Christian perfection. The apocryphal *Acts* of Paul, Peter, Thomas, Andrew, and John share a commitment to the superiority of sexual purity over the most pious marriage. Indeed, a passage from a fragment of John contains a diatribe against marriage that comes close to being totally unorthodox.[68] In the same book, the apostle gave thanks to the Lord for forcibly intervening to prevent his intended marriage and thus preserving his virginity.[69] *The Acts of Paul* incorporate a series of thirteen beatitudes of chastity. Rooted in the scanty remarks on the celibate life contained in Paul's Letter to the Corinthians, the author of the *Acts* concluded that without chastity there is no salvation.[70] In the *Acts of Peter,* the apostle's daughter preserved her virginity from an importunate suitor by lapsing into a permanent state of palsy, refusing her father's miraculous powers of healing.[71]

These stories presented the rejection of sexual activity, even in lawful marriage, as a heroic undertaking, a quest taken up by heroic women. The author of the *Acts of John* transformed the story of Drusiana and Callimachus from the *Satyricon* into a Christian tale. A chaste wife, having renounced her husband's bed, prayed successfully for death rather than submission to the violence of a seducer.[72] This story, with its complex ending featuring the resurrection of all the parties, continued to appeal strongly to women for many generations. In the tenth century, the playwriting nun, Hroswitha, used it for the plot of one of the plays she wrote to illustrate the heroism of chaste women in response to the contemporary vogue for the misogynistic plays of Terence.[73]

The *Acts of Thomas* contain a direct incitement to rebellion against the lot of women.[74] Converted by the apostle, the noble and beautiful Mygdonia took a vow to deny her husband his conjugal rights in the name of perfect chastity. When seduction and violence both failed to change her mind, the husband threatened to have Thomas executed, but Mygdonia would not relent. Indeed, she drew the King's wife and son into this nascent community of the chaste on a visit to Thomas in prison. At last, the exemplary death of the apostle caused the conversion of the King, the women were released from their connubial vows by their husbands, and all embarked on the chaste life. Less happy endings attended the story of Trophime, who was sentenced by her vengeful husband to a brothel, and Maximilla, whose brutal spouse was punished by a violent death without offspring.[75]

This ideal of Christian chastity as a device to liberate women from the sexual demands of their husbands was associated with the theme of virginity preserved from the "villainous" plots of parents. The most dramatic exemplar was Thecla, who was converted by Paul's preaching to the ideal of virginity and broke her betrothal, defying every parental effort to force her to honor the commitment.[76] Finally, her parents turned her over to the court to be executed for her refusal to marry. Escaping death not once, but twice, she embarked on a long career as a missionary. Despite her heroism she was refused baptism by Paul, and finally baptized herself while awaiting martyrdom. This puzzling event may reflect the reactions of women to the hesitation with which the clergy greeted their efforts to participate fully in the church. We have already seen that Tertullian felt the need to rebuke women who cited Thecla's example as justification for their own administration of the sacrament.

Though these tales are certainly fictional, we should not be too quick to dismiss them as mere melodramas in the mode of "The Perils of Pauline." The ideal they advanced was radical. The author of the *Acts of Thomas* maintained that a failure to bear children was a sign of merit, not a cause for grief as in the antique tradition.[77] The apostle Thomas preached that children gave few rewards in themselves, and that Jesus' command to leave home, family, possessions, and all to follow him was a command to renounce maternity.[78] We have already noted that these precepts ran counter to the laws of Rome and put women who followed them in danger of punishment by their fathers and the state. Moreover, there were women who actually did suffer the penalties of the law, as Justin Martyr reminded his readers around the middle of the century:

A certain woman lived with an intemperate husband; she herself had formerly been intemperate. But when she came to the knowledge of the teachings of Christ, she became soberminded and endeavored to persuade her husband, likewise to be temperate. . . . But he, continuing in the same excesses, alienated his wife from him by his actions. For she, considering it wicked to live any longer as a wife with a husband who sought in every way to indulge his pleasures contrary to the law of nature and in violation of what is right, wished to be divorced from him. And when she was over-persuaded by her friends, who advised her still to continue with him in the idea that some time or other her husband might give hope of amendment, she did violence to her own feelings and remained with him. But when her husband had gone into Alexandria and was reported to be conducting himself worse than ever, she . . . gave him a bill of divorce and was separated from him. But this noble husband of hers—while he ought to have been rejoicing that those actions which formerly she unhesitatingly committed with servants and hirelings, delighting in drunkenness and every vice, she had now given up, and desired that he too should give up the same—when she had gone from him without his desire, brought an accusation against her, affirming that she was a Christian.[79]

The woman's case was still outstanding when Justin wrote, but her Christian teacher and another of his more outspoken followers had already been executed. Yet in this case, the woman was not straying outside the expected boundaries of traditional classical morality. For those who defied the law itself in order to retain their virginity, there was no sanction in law or custom.

Yet we have seen that popular preachers who promoted the ideal of virginity or sexual abstinence after marriage commanded large followings of women. Representatives of the clergy, like Irenaeus of Lyon, condemned them for drawing women from their homes as well as for their heterodox theology. Indeed, as stable congregations became rooted in most of the great cities of the Empire, the need for wandering preachers gradually disappeared. Prophecy came into disrepute as doctrine hardened into orthodoxy. Irenaeus and his contemporaries undertook to establish the New Testament as a final and finished revelation to which nothing new would be added. They did not welcome ongoing revelation, even of the most orthodox nature. There is nothing in their writing in this period to suggest that they had engendered or even approved of the new and radical doctrines of chaste celibacy that appear in the apocrypha.

The message that women should forsake husbands, homes, and children for the sake of sexual purity was not received well by the clergy. For one thing, they generally favored a return to the older values of family life. Nor had they yet solved the problem of establishing an alternative life for such women. On the contrary, they were increasingly less welcoming to women who wanted to devote their time to religious service. Nevertheless, from the apocryphal to the heretical, the prophetic daughters of the second-century church preached a deep distrust of the flesh, a profound asceticism that rejected sexual activity and childbearing and the whole social definition of women based on biological and gender-related functions.

We have no way of estimating the numbers of these women or of their followers. They were numerous and influential enough to be considered dangerous by the greatest churchmen of the day. They threatened to plunge the church into schism at the very moment when a Roman Emperor was determined to extirpate it from his realm. In the face of this threat, the clerical hierarchy chose accommodation as the price of their loyalty, as long as their ideals were not rooted in gnostic cosmology. For the first time in history, women with roles outside the family structure claimed a life of adventure in the service of a new religion. The result would ultimately be the restructuring of the whole social order.

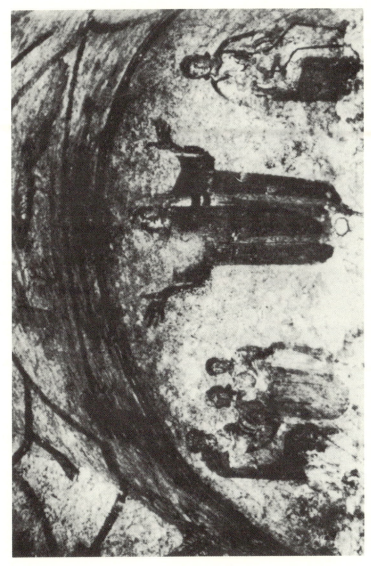

FIGURE 5. The veiled Virgin: Veiling ceremony at right; mother and child at left. Rome, Catacomb of Priscilla. From Grabar, André, *Early Christian Art* (New York: Odyssey Press, 1968), plate 115.

Chapter Five:
And I Became a Man

Until the reign of Marcus Aurelius, Christians lived in an uneasy truce with their pagan neighbors. Outbursts of local hostility were sporadic, localized, and soon over. Despite the personal dangers, Christians married pagans. They converted the children of pagan parents. Slaves or their owners were often Christian. Christians and pagans were companions in all the common pursuits of daily life. The process of conversion, therefore, worked as a solvent on the barriers of age, sex, status, and nationality that constituted the Roman social structure.

By the end of the second century, the Emperor was apparently convinced that the religion posed a serious threat to the moral foundations of his society. A widespread persecution was launched. In 177, in Lyon, a slave girl named Blandina died in the same arena with her mistress; the congregation of Irenaeus of Lyon circulated a letter to other communities in the Empire acknowledging the girl's heroism, which had transcended all the disabilities of her mortal condition:

> But the entire fury of the crowd, governor and soldiers fell on . . . Blandina, through whom Christ showed that things which appear mean and unsightly and despicable in the eyes of men are accounted worthy of great glory in the sight of God, through love towards Him, a love which showed itself in power and did not boast itself in appearance. For when we were all afraid, and her mistress according to the flesh (who was herself also a combatant in the ranks of the martyrs) was in a state of agony, lest the weakness of her body should render her unable even to make a bold confession, Blandina was filled with such power that those who by turns kept torturing her in every way from dawn to evening were worn out and exhausted and themselves confessed defeat from lack of aught else to do

to her; they marvelled that the breath still remained in a body all mangled and covered with gaping wounds, and they testified that a single form of torture was sufficient to render life extinct, let alone such and so many. But the blessed woman, like a noble champion, in confession regained her youth; and for her to say, "I am a Christian, and with us evil finds no place," was refreshment and rest and insensibility to her lot.[1]

The Martyrs of Lyon vividly demonstrated the cohesion of women and men, slaves and owners, that represented the highest ideals of Christianity. In the face of imperial persecution, orthodox leaders could no longer countenance the tendency of some of their members to drift into segregated sects. To unite their communities in this emergency, they needed, among other things, a Christian program for the conduct of family and sexual relationships. They had to recognize the presence of the celibate in their midst and to formulate a social vision which would incorporate their experiences. Martyrdom, with its attendant imagery of athletic competition and military strife, was soon to be recognized as a transcendental victory over the physical conditions of mortality. It was the ultimate act of salvation where, mystically, women became men.[2]

The Reintegration of the Christian Community

Celibate Christian women of the first and second centuries supplemented and possibly even supplanted the organized liturgy directed by the male clergy with a religious life centered on the services of deaconesses and the teaching of itinerant prophets and prophetesses. We can only conjecture about the self-perceptions of these women. Certainly their circumstances made a certain amount of redefinition inescapable.

First, since they were not married or living in quasi-marital relationships with men, their lives were not defined or structured in terms of conjugality. Family patterns may have dominated the lives of younger women, who still enjoyed a filial relationship to their fathers or of widows with young children. But as they grew older, the importance of these relationships must have diminished. The celibate woman who had renounced her sexuality inevitably moved steadily away from the male figures who would normally have supplied the defining "self" to her "other."

Second, the apocryphal literature suggests what the careers of the prophetesses known to us confirms: at least some of these women saw themselves as the active leaders of their communities. They set the pattern against which others, both men and women, reacted. These women were not necessarily subject to the decisions of the clerical hierarchy, since there was as yet no machinery by which the orthodox clergy could secure submission to their direction. Indeed, the Christian faith contained no inherent need for clerical administration: it was the clergy's own desire for unity and uniformity that brought it about. Bishops and priests had determined not to include women in their ranks in this period, but they still had to persuade women, particularly the celibate among them, to recognize their authority.

Between the persecutions of Marcus Aurelius in the 170s and those of the Severi in the 220s, two generations of male apologists were preoccupied with the task of procuring doctrinal and administrative unity among Christians. Orthodox apologists, like Irenaeus and Hippolytus of Rome, sought to demolish heterodox sects. In Alexandria, Clement and Origen laid the foundations of a systematic Christian theology.[3] Justin and Tertullian contributed ethical treatises to secure Christian conformity, not only to Gospel teachings, but to some of the moral standards of the Roman world as well. By publishing a full account of Christian lives and manners, the apologists hoped to convert imperial officials to a more favorable view of their co-religionists. The discipline of excommunication was combined with the persuasions of theology to establish and impose a more coherent set of norms on the faithful. To be successful, however, the church had to take account of the needs and wishes of communicants, as long as they did not conflict irredeemably with evangelical teaching.

The clergy were aware of the value of educated aristocratic women to their cause. Marcia, the mistress of Commodus, was credited with persuading his father, Marcus Aurelius, to end his persecution. In the next generation, the Empress Julia Mammaea invited Origen to instruct her in the principles of religion.[4] Though he failed to convert her or the other women of the Severan family, the incident must have reinforced the general resolve of Christian teachers to pay attention to the instruction of their female catechumens.

Another reason for the apologists to address women was their anxiety that untrained females might be the weak link in the chain of resistance to the persecutors. Eusebius stressed that church leaders in Lyon were nervous about the examination of Blandina and her sisters, since they might prove to be "manifestly unready for martyrdom and untrained and still weak and unable to bear the strain of mighty conflict."[5] Such a one was Biblis, whose courage initially failed her. But when she saw the torments of her companions she remembered the threat of eternal punishment in Hell and joined them in their triumph.[6] At least one of the six students of Origen who were captured and martyred in the renewed persecution of 204 was a woman.[7]

In the light of the emergency caused by the persecutions, Blandina's contemporary, Clement of Alexandria, viewed the independent Christian women of his city with dismay. Their religious life seemed to him to be appallingly free of supervision. He turned a bilious eye on the communities of Christian women, claiming that their members had somehow strayed far from their shepherd and his flock. He said they spent their days travelling through the streets in litters, stopping to chat with friends as they went from one temple to another. Nor did he see their devotion to churchgoing as evidence of piety. He feared they spent their time there practicing divination, hob-nobbing with disreputable priests and learning charms and incantations from a collection of old women.[8]

Nor was Clement's anxiety lessened when he contemplated the women who stayed peaceably in their houses. He maintained that crowds of unsavory people flowed in and out, giggling and whispering and exposing Christian women to all sorts of scandal. Clement, like many a later sermonizer, was given to rather lurid descriptions of the lives of his readers. However, he must have been genuinely disturbed by a population of wealthy and influential women instructed by other women and itinerant preachers of both genders. The solution, he saw, was to bring women back under the more generalized instruction of approved representatives of the church.

Clement wrote several extensive books of moral instruction. In one, *Paedagogus* (or, as the most recent translation has it, *Christ the Educator*), he presented his views within the extended metaphor of children under the guidance of their pedagogue, claiming firmly that "men and women alike are under the pedagogue's charge."[9] His views were grounded in the idea that women and men were equal in the Christian life, at least spiritually. Clement argued that women and men should be subjected to a single moral standard and a single rule of individual responsibility:[10]

The virtue of men and women is the same. For if the God of both is one, the master of both is also one; one church, one temperance, one modesty; their food is common, marriage an equal yoke; respiration, sight, hearing, knowledge, hope, obedience, love, all alike. And those whose life is common have common grace and a common salvation; common to them are love and training.[11]

He went on to illustrate the equal requirements for decorous dress, temperate manners, and modest behavior to be imposed on persons of both sexes, though he would allow women to dress in softer materials and stouter shoes than the rougher physiques of men required. He advised both men and women to bathe and get proper physical exercise. However, he admonished them against bathing together in the seductive atmosphere of the public bathhouse and advised them to get their exercise in honest toil. In the matter of work, Clement apparently assumed that the sexual division of labor would be maintained, though elsewhere he pointed out that men could manage houses if they had to and women had been known to take up arms, although "Christians do not train our women like Amazons to manliness in war, since we wish even our men to be peaceable."[12] To be sure, he did not uniformly maintain this high plane; more than once, he cited the Pauline letters urging women to submit to their husbands.

On the other hand, he decidedly turned against the trend toward segregation in the Egyptian church. He wanted to woo women away from the unsupervised gatherings that disturbed him so much. He urged that they be integrated into a congregation where they would attend services on an equal basis with men, though suitably dressed as formulated in the Pauline prescriptions:

Woman and man are to go to church decently attired, with natural step embracing silence, possessing unfeigned love, pure in body and pure in heart, fit to pray to God. Let the woman observe this further. Let her be entirely covered unless she happens to be at home. For that type of dress is grave and protects her from being gazed at. . . . For this is the wish of the Lord, since it is becoming for her to pray veiled.[13]

Apparently, Clement opposed the Egyptian practice of putting a wall between women and men; he was more interested in getting women into the church and integrating them into the flock. Nor was he alone. *The Apostolic Constitutions,* compiled at a somewhat later date, also display some anxiety about getting women to attend church services on a regular basis. They firmly deny the excuses used by women to separate themselves from the community or neglect participating in the Eucharist:

> Now, if any persons keep to the Jewish customs. . .let them tell us whether in those hours or days when they undergo any such thing, they observe not to pray or touch a Bible or partake of the Eucharist. . . .For, if thou thinkest, O woman, when thou art seven days in thy separation, that thou art void of the Holy Spirit, then if thou shouldst die suddenly thou wilt depart void of the spirit. . . .But thou standest in need of prayer and the Eucharist, and the coming of the Holy Spirit, as having been guilty of no fault in this matter. For neither lawful mixture, nor child-bearing, nor the menstrual purgation, nor nocturnal pollution can define the nature of a man, or separate the Holy Spirit from him.[14]

This imposition of a single moral standard and a single liturgical custom for the entire laity was designed to produce two results: all Christians would be brought into regular communion with one another which would strengthen their cohesiveness as a church, and all would submit uniformly to the sacramental authority of the clergy. Clement further hoped to impose a standard of sober custom on women and men alike in their behavior outside of church services. Even when he launched diatribes against feminine vanity which echoed Juvenal and other pagan contemporaries in their satirical power, he expected women to read his work and he tried earnestly to persuade them of his point of view. No doubt this explains why his moral objections to artifice and luxury were mixed with warnings that hair dye hastens the natural graying of the hair and cosmetics ultimately dry and wrinkle the skin. Like Tertullian at the end of this period, Clement hoped to persuade women to take instruction from male teachers, but he could not force them to do so.

In the long run, the effort appears to have been successful. Christian women ultimately were wooed away from the circles of prophetesses and heretical leaders of both genders into a more conservatively established church. To understand this ultimate success, we must look at the Christian ideas on familial and celibate ways of living as they evolved around the beginning of the third century after Christ.

The Family Redefined

Condemning the bizarre sexual teachings of some heterodox Christians, Justin Martyr claimed that the orthodox subscribed to no exotic or unsavory practices: ''But whether we marry, it is only that we may bring up children; or whether we decline marriage, we live continently.''[15] Clement of Alexandria's vision of Christian morality was, superficially at least, even more conformable to the standards of classical Rome. He was probably a married man himself and regarded the celibate with contempt. To him, chastity meant simply marital fidelity, a prudent and modest fulfillment of love between two virtuous people. He defined continence as the restraint of unbridled lust in favor of a rational and honorable connubial union. Clement employed the tools of sharp social satire against the lax social behavior of his contemporaries: excessive luxury in dress, drunkenness, overeating, and sexual indulgence. In this, however, he went no further than Juvenal and other pagan moral critics. His condemnation of serial monogamy through divorce ran counter to the permissiveness of Roman Law but was far from offensive to the ethical sentiments of pagans. Unlike some of his more radical contemporaries, he also urged the remarriage of the widowed.[16]

Clement's views on marriage, however, reflected Christian sentiments which were radical in the purest sense of the word. They differed fundamentally from pagan attitudes in their conceptions of the purposes and functions of the family. Classical philosophers saw the family as the foundation of the state, the building block for the entire political superstructure. The softening of the *patria potestas,* evident in classical Roman Law, ultimately operated only to the advantage of husbands within the conjugal unit; it did not lessen the subjection of women and children or bring them closer to an autonomous role in public life. To some extent, Christian ideas on the family had a similar development. Justin, Clement, and Tertullian agreed that the Christian family was based only upon the relationship of the conjugal couple and their minor children, cutting away the influence of the great *familia* with its paternal power. Though Clement subscribed to Paul's view that women should obey their husbands, he tended to view the family as a unit rather than a hierarchy. He interpreted Jesus' promise, ''Wherever two or three are gathered together in my name, there am I," as an endorsement of the Christian family. He saw the conjugal pair and their children as a complete congregation.[17]

Within marriage, Clement envisioned women as fulfilling the traditional roles of housekeeper and child-rearer. However, he argued for equal balance in the marital relationship to ensure the chaste union that befitted a congregation. He put all his authority behind the argument that the couple should be equal in age and other social characteristics. He went so far as to declare that parents who forced an immature girl into marriage were guilty of fornication because they could not assure her willing participation.[18] Where Roman jurists propounded the consensual marriage based upon the man's will, Clement stressed the importance of the woman's will to ensure a bride "who does not by force of compulsion love the husband who loves her."[19] The woman's consent and maturity were vital to his concept of marriage because a woman's obedience to her husband's judgment was always to be tempered by the moral imperatives dictated by her quest for salvation.

Tertullian, in the next generation, was even more explicitly at odds with the principles of Roman law, which sought to respect and protect class divisions and noble lineages. He argued that Christian women should put aside social and economic considerations in favor of a community of faith in marriage. Apparently, he believed that women were free to do this without being checked by parents or guardians. Perhaps below the ranks of the great senatorial families there was more individual freedom of choice than we generally believe. Or possibly Christian parents had already been disciplined to bow before the choices of their children, provided the choices were morally sound. Certainly, Tertullian viewed his own marriage in that light and wrote enthusiastically to his wife:

> How beautiful, then, the marriage of two Christians: two who are one in hope, one in desire, one in the way of life they follow, one in the religion they practice. They are as brother and sister, both servants of the same master. Nothing divides them, either in flesh or in spirit. They are, in very truth, two in one flesh: and where there is but one flesh, there is also but one spirit. They pray together, they worship together, they fast together; instructing one another, encouraging one another, strengthening one another. Side by side, they visit God's

church and partake of God's banquet; side by side, they face difficulties and persecution, share their consolations. They have no secrets from one another and never shun each other's company; they never bring sorrow to each other's hearts. Unembarrassed they visit the sick and assist the needy. They give alms without anxiety; they attend the Sacrifice without difficulty; they perform their daily exercises of piety without hindrance. They need not be furtive about making the Sign of the Cross, nor timorous in greeting the brethren, nor silent in asking the blessing of God. Psalms and hymns they sing to one another, striving to see which one of them will chant more beautifully the praises of the Lord. Hearing and seeing this, Christ rejoices. To such as these he gives his peace. Where there are two together, there also he is present; and where he is, evil is not.[20]

Tertullian's reiteration of Clement's vision of the family as a congregation underscores the unity of their effort. Certainly neither theologian saw the husband in the place of the clergy in this congregation but, rather, placed the leadership directly in Christ.

In practice, a good Christian marriage, emptied of its religious content, would not seem incompatible with pagan moral precepts. The theoretical differences between the two, however, were significant. For example, Christians disregarded the family's function as a juridical or economic unit. Furthermore, the claims of religion were expected to triumph incontestably in any conflict with the claims of society. Thus, marriage was a more conjugal-centered enterprise than even the most modern trends in Roman law allowed. The wife's father had no authoritative role in its conduct, whereas her own consent was indispensable to its formation. As a congregation, the famiy unit was expected to abide by rules of decorum which included wifely deference to the head of the family. But the father/ husband was displaced from his role at the head of the congregation: each individual was reoriented toward a relationship that faced outward to Christ and, ultimately, to salvation.

This reorientation explains the egalitarian elements in Clement's approach to the problem of gender. Clement viewed the differences between women and men as strictly limited to the physiological functions necessary for procreation. ''Pregnancy and parturition belong to a woman as she is a woman and not as she is a human being,'' he claimed. The peculiar construction of a woman's body had no bearing on her moral nature, nor on her religious responsibilities:

> As far as respects human nature, the woman does not possess one nature and the man exhibit another, but the same: so also with virtue. If, consequently, a self-restraint and righteousness and whatever qualities are regarded as following them, is the virtue of the male, it would belong to the male alone to be virtuous and to the woman to be licentious and unjust. But it is offensive even to say this. Accordingly, women are to practice self-restraint and righteousness and every other virtue, as well as men, both bond and free; since it is a fit consequence that the same nature possesses one and the same virtue.[21]

Clement sought a social vision that would bring the religious women of Alexandria back from the congregations led by "old women'' (probably deaconesses and consecrated widows) into the fold of the clerical shepherds who strove to direct the religious life of all Christians. Within his relatively conservative view of the social structure, he had begun to carve out a space for the individuality of women; beneath the smooth surface of the *familia,* he saw a group of morally autonomous individuals. This recognition of women's responsibility for their own salvation and their capacities for spiritual excellence brought them, at least partially, out from under the authority of their husbands and fathers and attached them to the authority of clerical instructors instead. It is clear that Clement's ideals do not add up to a very extensive program of liberation for women. Yet, this call for women's submission to an extrafamilial authority was a recognition of their existence as individuals.

Clement's assertion that women were morally equal to men and his insistence that they be held responsible for their own religious lives was intrinsic to his defense of orthodoxy. He did not extend this view as far as did his radical contemporaries, however. He did not endorse the celibate way of life for women or for men. The women he hoped to woo back to the congregation were probably susceptible to the teachings of Encratites and other heretics who condemned marriage, procreation, and all the works of the flesh. Clement despised the Encratites, likening them to the hypocrites who called Jesus a wine-bibber.[22] He accused the celibate of lovelessness, "letting the fires of charity die.''[23]

He maintained that his rivals had no respect for women's independence despite their opposition to traditional conjugal morality, which apparently attracted a female following. Indeed, he violently condemned them for freeing women from marriage only to treat them as property. He charged that sects which initially preached equality tended, in the end, to share women in common among male adherents—a criticism that has more than once been levelled at the modern "sexual revolution."[24] Clement hoped to turn Christian women away from "false prophets" who pretended that their spiritual superiority had released them from the moral restraints imposed on ordinary folk.[25] He maintained that they would find true freedom within the framework of Christian marriage, where they would be subject only to the law of God.

Clement's idea of marriage was, therefore, a union of two individuals seeking a Christian life. The authority of husbands was to be limited. Wives could not plead that authority to excuse their own spiritual delinquencies, but must defy their husbands when necessary and exert their own moral authority where they could. "It is noble for a man to die for virtue and for liberty and for himself, and so also it is for a woman."[26] Even where it was not a question of martyrdom, each individual was expected to pursue her own good and her own salvation: "it is not in the power of any other" to restrain her.[27]

This view of marriage could cause problems for a Christian woman married to a pagan. Recognizing their situation, Clement relaxed his prescriptions concerning dress and cosmetics "for women who have not been fortunate in falling in with chaste husbands and adorn themselves in order to please their husbands."[28] Wives of pagans could charm their husbands by their dress and manners, though he always hoped that they would "allay by degrees the irrational impulses and passions of their husbands. And they are to be gently drawn to simplicity by gradually accustoming them to sobriety."[29]

In his own musings on the problems of marriage, Tertullian considered the dilemma of a woman caught between the obligations of marriage and the unseemly demands of her husband and found it almost insoluble. Pagan husbands would almost inevitably have made demands that ran counter to the Christian duties of their wives. They could order them to join the family in celebrating pagan festivals. They might even demand that their unwilling wives display their bodies immodestly in public. And the wives risked their lives if they sought to evade these commands. He bitterly pointed out that the most tolerant husband was a dangerous repository for his wife's secret: in making her husband her confidante, the Christian wife gave him a weapon in reserve if ever he should be moved to turn against her.[30]

The happy solution, naturally, was exemplified in the tale of Saint Cecilia, who converted her husband on her wedding day and persuaded him to join her in a life of mutual chastity. Their joint martyrdom ultimately crowned this victory. In reality, however, a husband would more likely have joined in the persecution of his wife, as in the case cited by Justin or, a century later, the case of Bona, "who was dragged by her husband to sacrifice, who did not pollute her conscience, but, as those holding her hands sacrificed, began to cry out against it: 'I have not done it! You have done it!' "[31]

As the champion of marriage and family life, Clement had attempted to promote a partnership of spouses which provided for the spiritual responsibilities of married women. However, the conflict between this ideal and the highly structured *familia* of antiquity was tragically exposed when a woman kept her faith at the cost of her life. Moreover, the individualist philosophy inherent in Christian morality inevitably led many Christians, female and male, to a concept of self that was not limited by relationships to other human beings. Clement was the last Christian writer to argue for a society in which all but the most unfortunate and incidental individuals would be grouped in familial congregations. Origen, who succeeded him as head of the Alexandrian school, was so determined to transcend the constraints of the gender system that he castrated himself, interpreting literally Jesus' remarks concerning those who make themselves eunuchs for the sake of heaven. In Africa, Tertullian became so convinced that marriage was a bond transcending sexuality that he became a heretic rather than admit the legitimacy of "digamy." The women who were the objects of so much of their teaching remain silent, but their deeds still speak to us. They were already dedicating themselves to lives outside of marriage. It remained only for the leaders in the making of Christian theology to recognize their existence and supply a plausible theoretical framework for them. Over these two generations, Christian apologists slowly altered their conception of the social structure so as to provide a special niche for the unmarried, particularly the unmarried woman, a species of being which had formerly seemed beyond the capacity of logic to imagine.

The Celibate Orders

Celibacy has always been the unsought fate of many women, but the subjects of this study are a select group who chose the celibate life, who modelled themselves after the heroines of the apocryphal gospels. These virgins were not simply young unmarried females but women determined never to marry and never to surrender their physical integrity. We know few of them by name but occasionally the memory of her martyrdom has preserved one or two from oblivion. Thus Potamiaena, martyred in the early third century, who converted her executioner through visions after her death, was still famous in the countryside a century later. Tradition recounted her energetic defense of her virginity against countless suitors and, finally, against her lustful jailors, when she and her mother, Marcella, were cast into prison. Indeed, her judge threatened to turn her over to the gladiators for their entertainment and she escaped only by uttering "profanity" sufficiently strong to induce him to have her killed on the spot.[32] Cecilia, martyred between 177 and 180, retained her virginity by converting her husband on their wedding night. Felicity, who was executed in Rome in 162 for successfully preaching Christianity in public and converting many of her listeners, was a widow vowed to continence.

Widows, even consecrated widows, had been known in the church since Paul's time. Though he had wished to restrict their numbers to a few elderly women, many churchmen in the early third century began to see them as a growing and desirable component in the Christian congregation. Tertullian, who is known to have been influenced in the matter by Montanist prophetesses, left the orthodox church rather than give up his belief that a widowed Christian should never remarry. His difficulties are indicative of those experienced by the Fathers in arriving at a comprehensive vision of a celibate order despite the existence of growing numbers of celibates.

Tertullian was the first Christian to attempt the structuring of a celibate order. In his letter to his wife, he described three ranks: those who were devoted to perpetual virginity from birth; those who determined to embrace "virginity" from the moment of their rebirth in baptism (a group who might not be celibates but vowed to continence within marriage); those who turned away from remarriage when widowhood gave them a second chance for "virginity":

Although virgins, because of their perfect integrity and in-

violate purity, will look upon the face of God most closely, yet
the life a widow leads is the more difficult since it is easy not to
desire that of which you are ignorant and easy to turn your
back upon what you have never desired. Chastity is most
praiseworthy when it is sensible of the right it has sacrificed
and knows what it has experienced. The condition of virgin
may be regarded as one of greater felicity, but that of the
widow is one of greater difficulty; the former has always
possessed the good, the latter had to find it on her own. In the
former, it is the grace which is crowned; in the latter, virtue.[33]

This is the first full-scale argument in favor of virginity and chaste
widowhood made by a patristic writer. But it was written by a man
well on his way to excommunication, one who was far from expressing an orthodox ideal to be imposed on female communicants.
In fact, he was trying to give order and clarity to a way of life that
many of them had already adopted for themselves.

Other ideals, with roots in the Apocrypha, began to appear in the
writings of the Fathers at this time. For example, the implications of
Mary's virginity began to interest writers in the mainstream.[34]
Thus, ideas we noted among the partially segregated circles of
devout women in the second century began to circulate among the
fathers as they attempted to reintegrate these women back into their
fold. There is no way for us to know how successful the effort was
at the turn of the third century. Many women who had moved into
heterodox circles and flourished as prophetesses would have been
totally impervious to their appeal. But for women who were uncon-
vinced by Clement's warm defence of Christian marriage, or whom
chance had deprived of its comforts, the honor that the church began
to pay to celibates must have been very attractive.

Nevertheless, we should view this move with considerable caution. When women were the chief practitioners of chaste celibacy,
the orthodox did not promote it as a desirable way of life. During the
first two centuries there undoubtedly were male virgins and
widowers, but their failure to marry did not appear so threatening to
the natural order of things. It was the unmarried woman who provoked notice. But in the early third century, male writers began to
address themselves to questions of male celibacy. At the middle of
the century, Cyprian of Carthage apparently thought that he had to
point out that women as well as men might be qualified as virgins of
the church.[35]

Though the practitioners of celibacy must have been drawn to their life by its positive attractions, the literature on the subject is often marked by the negative images of revulsion from sexuality and from the opposite sex in general. In the apocryphal gospels, as I noted in the last chapter, this revulsion was most commonly against the male sex. Men are viewed as lustful, brutal oppressors before whom tender maidens and gentle wives recoil, turning to the promise of another world for escape. This provides one of the strongest arguments for believing that much of this literature was written by women or at least for them by sympathetic men. The terrible tales of the virgin martyrs threatened with rape as well as physical torture are suffused with the same fear of the male sex. With the promulgation of male virginity, however, a note of misogyny was introduced into the literature. It was a note still fairly rare in the period under consideration, but one destined to grow in later centuries. In the third century, Tertullian, like a Christian Juvenal, condemned women in one of his heterodox tracts as ''the devil's gateway.''[36]

The forces of orthodoxy were increasingly successful in combatting the anti-sexual ideals of many gnostic sects. They refused to admit the flesh as the creation of the devil. They insisted that Jesus was a man of flesh and that he was born of a woman, though the idea of his mother as a perpetual virgin was gaining ground. Prophecy fell into disrepute and, with it, not only the diversity of early Christian preaching but also the teaching role of women.

But, stripped of the heretical material of gnostic teaching, the ideal of purity, of a single-minded dedication to the service of God excluding the distractions of home and family, remained powerful. Even as the celibate prophets receded in importance, the idea began to circulate among the clergy that celibacy was a superior state. One of the first effects of this sentiment, however, was the implicit denigration of the priest's wife. By the middle of the third century, Cyprian's praise of a priest's wife who joined her husband in martyrdom was exceptional.[37] The *Apostolic Constitutions* of that period prohibited clergy from marrying women who had been servants, courtesans, widows, or divorcées, but provided no positive prescriptions for these wives.[38]

In fact, they decreed that the office of deaconess was to be restricted to virgins or ''at least, a widow who has been but once married, faithful and well-esteemed.''[39] Thus a role within the church, however restricted, was beginning to be envisioned for the celibate woman but not for the married one. Even a priest's wife would have to wait for her husband's death to qualify as a deaconess, and even then, as a widow, she would have to take second place to a virgin. The prescription of celibacy was advanced more strongly for widowed clergymen.

As taken over by male writers in this period, the discussion of celibacy returned to the old Pauline vision associating it with liberty to pursue the evangelical mission. Assuredly, the revival of the vision of the Christian as one unencumbered by all social ties must be associated with the escalating danger of the renewed persecutions rather than with the ideal of a new way of life. Early in the period, Clement had opposed the celibate prophets in favor of the settled and married clergy, pointing out that the majority of the apostles had been helped by their wives.[40] Indeed, he felt that celibacy condemned men to the selfishness and coldness of a solitary life which in the end would breed hatred of humanity and freeze the fires of love.[41] If preachers felt that their mission required sexual continence, he advised them to have wives as though they had them not, following the Pauline suggestion. These wives could minister among women in their houses without scandal. But this was a losing battle. Justin Martyr had long since pointed out that many Christians, both men and women, "who have been Christ's disciples from childhood, remain pure at the age of sixty or seventy years."[42]

Even Clement was persuaded that Paul's command that bishops and deacons must be husbands of "one wife" meant that they must remain unmarried if widowed. (although he tried to emphasize that Paul was simply confirming Jesus' prohibition against divorce.) Even Origen, whose auto-castration brought him the recurring censure by the episcopal establishment reflected the general perplexity on the subject. If, as Origen supposed, Paul thought that the discipline of self-denial and chastity would improve a clergyman's character, why would he countenance the retention of a single wife through a long life, but bar that man who may have lost two wives in succession while still young?[43]

Origen was the first and most famous of the churchmen who espoused celibacy and total chastity as a more direct route to perfection than marriage. He was a young man in the Alexandria of ascetic heretics like Julius Cassianus, whom Clement had criticized at some length.[44] Like many of the heretics, he was involved in teaching young women and may have wished to ensure that he could not be touched by scandal. Strange as it seems to us today, his contemporaries felt that stern disciplinary steps were needed to ensure that others would not imitate his self-mutilation to ensure their purity.[45]

Though he accepted Paul's command that clergymen be husbands, Origen suggested that they should not have children.[46] Contemporary bishops, who were married, were apparently subjected to even greater pressures. Polycratus of Ephesus felt compelled to write to Victor of Rome about 190 to justify the family tradition that made him the eighth member of his family to succeed to the bishopric of Ephesus.[47] Pope Callixtus (217-222) was severely criticized for his decision to maintain married clerks in their functions.[48] By the middle of the third century, the *Didascalia* tried to limit the numbers of the married clergy in episcopal offices without contraverting the Pauline prescription, by attempting to impose a rule that men under fifty would not be installed in the office. It also attempted to prevent the clergy from marrying after they had taken office, even if they had never been married before.[49]

In summary, the idea that celibacy was a more perfect state than marriage was gaining ground. The clergy, accordingly, made some moves in the direction of becoming a celibate order though, in fact, the habit and appeal of married life proved too strong to break. Among celibate men, only Origen sought to deny and transcend his masculinity by a violent gesture that attracted loud condemnation and a few emulators. Origen's mutilation was put forward as a barrier to his ordination. Indeed, eunuchs in general were barred from the masculine clergy even when their castration had not been of their own choosing.

With the failure of the move to clerical celibacy and the reaffirmation of the masculine quality of the clerical order, the unmarried Christian who sought a way of life that transcended gender was placed in a highly ambiguous position. On the one hand, there was a growing body of opinion, even among male theologians, that celibacy was a superior way of life. These writers readily recognized the presence and even the leadership of women among the celibates and made efforts to secure them for the orthodox congregations. Yet, these women were barred from the offices that governed the church.

Long before, Paul had said that in Christ there was neither male nor female. In a sense, Clement of Alexandria was pursuing the same idea when he argued that women were women only in their sexual and procreative functions and in the social roles which stemmed from those functions. Clement, of course, was not anxious to cope with the intellectual problem raised by women who eschewed those roles, for he wanted all his flock to marry. Indeed, when he was confronted with Paul's ideal, he tried to dispose of it lamely, by applying the allegorical approach to scripture which he had pioneered in other contexts. Faced with the apocryphal and quasi-gnostic *Gospel to the Egyptians,* in which the Lord prophesied to Salome, "You will trample underfoot the garment of shame, when the two are made one, masculine and feminine, neither male nor female," Clement gave it a symbolic meaning. He claimed that it meant simply that the female vice of cupidity and the male vice of anger would be overcome by the female virtue of modesty and the male virtue of reason.[50]

This device received no serious attention from anyone. The pressures in favor of celibacy, particularly celibacy for women, were growing stronger. In the shadow of persecution, they were irresistible. By the early third century, the gnostic threat was largely receding and the practitioners of celibacy did not need to justify themselves in the light of esoteric doctrines concerning the creation of the flesh. But those who embraced the celibate life were deliberately and self-consciously entering a new social structure in which some women, by Clement's definition, ceased to be women. What, then, could they be? In effect, they answered, they could become classificatory men.

If women were defined by marriage, by its sexual and procreative roles and by the gender-based labor assigned to married women, then their refusal of marriage might move them into a category that transcended womanhood. Mary had once chosen "the better part" in preferring spiritual instruction to domestic duties. Tertullian effectively defended her choice when he condemned the whole notion of the sexual division of labor as a justification for marriage. He agreed that there was great convenience in arranging work in this manner but he scoffed at those who did not think that a man could keep a house or do his own bookkeeping. He growled that a woman's desire to queen it over a man's household might lead a widow to remarry, but it was entirely unnecessary.[51]

Only in the arena of martyrdom can we view these transcendent women unfiltered by the lenses of male observers. We have already noted the determination with which virgin martyrs defended their integrity. From the early third century, we have one piece of direct testimony from a woman who, although not a virgin, put all the traits of womanhood behind her as she faced an overwhelming spiritual imperative.

Perpetua, a Roman matron, faced the lions with her former slave, Felicity, in Carthage on March 7, 203. While awaiting her execution, she recorded the dreams and anxieties she experienced in prison, which finally led her to a new vision of herself in which all her mortal persona was burned away. An unknown spectator, possibly Tertullian, rescued these documents from oblivion and appended an eyewitness account of the women's death. The result is an authentic female voice recording the emergence of her autonomous spiritual being from the cocoon of her womanhood.

Both Perpetua and Felicity were married and, at the time of their execution, they were both new mothers. Perpetua described the urgency of Felicity's prayers that she be delivered in time to join her companions in the trials of the arena. Her prayers were rewarded by a premature birth. Both women surrendered their babies, the most pressing ties to their womanhood, a few days before death. Perpetua described the pains in her breasts from the receding milk which so painfully symbolized the nature of her metamorphosis.

Step by step, Perpetua had renounced everything that made her a woman and a matron. Her husband does not figure at all in the tale of her passion; it seems that she was already irremediably estranged from him. But she was still in conflict with her pagan parents who begged her to recant and return home with them. At last she convinced them that she was obdurate and they left, bearing her baby with them.

Perpetua stripped away the emotions and the constraints of the feminine role she had once fully played. She was tormented by dreams and visions that reflected the agony of her soul in this ordeal. On the night before her execution, she dreamed that she had entered into the arena to fight the beasts. There she was confronted by a "certain ill-favored Egyptian" who challenged her to fight with him. "Also, there came to me comely young men, my helpers and aiders. And I was stripped, and I became a man. . . ."[52]

FIGURE 6. Orant with group of women. Rome, Sarcophagus, Museo Laterano. From Grabar, André, *Early Christian Art* (New York: Odyssey Press, 1968), plate 145.

Chapter Six: Singing the New Song

Perpetua's dream that she had become a man expressed her personal sense of loss and transformation, her awareness that she was gradually moving away from her life as a woman toward a final transcendent experience. Her final ordeal also vibrantly expressed the Pauline formula, "neither bond nor free, male nor female." Perpetua's life as a man was brief and circumscribed to the contest of the arena; but throughout the third century her renunciation of the womanly life was repeated by growing numbers of women who were neither imprisoned nor martyred.

The bulk of our information about these women comes from the African church where Perpetua had lived and died, though it is clear that similar communities flourished at least from Asia Minor to Africa. This same period saw the final success of the episcopal hierarchy in integrating and organizing the church under its direction. This is the context in which the final act of our drama is set: the admission of a community of celibate women into the social structure of Christianity.

Orthodox writers of the early third century were concerned for the first time with the problem of imposing discipline on these women and defining their appropriate place in the congregation. In Perpetua's age and in the next generation, female virgins were actively challenging traditional gender roles in Christian communities. Though it is clear that men also embraced the life of asexual celibacy, Christian writers do not appear to have perceived them as a challenge to the order of their communities. Since a full range of roles, from pious layman to bishop, was open to men, and a growing party within the church accepted and even championed the idea of clerical celibacy, male virgins could be readily integrated into the community at every level. Male theologians, however, had serious difficulties in adapting their social and clerical ideas to the existence of celibate women as active components of their congregations.

Virile Women

The women who formed the celibate groups to whom third-century theologians gave their attention were not heretical. There is no evidence that they took the extreme gnostic positions that condemned the flesh and all its procreative works or even that they sought to take up priestly roles in heterodox congregations. However, they were probably inspired by the heroines of the apocryphal literature in formulating a conception of virginity as a way of life. The rejection of sexual activity was, obviously, but the beginning of their adventure. By leaving husbands, rejecting marriage, or even living in continence with their husbands, they were throwing off the usual responsibilities of the Roman matron. As independent persons, they were shaping lives outside the normal patterns of social authority and taking for themselves the autonomous personality that Roman Law still reserved only for mothers of three or four children.

In a very practical sense, this is what it meant to "become a man." Women who did not live as women had to take on some of the mundane functions of men in managing the basic mechanics of their own lives. As we shall see, they also sought to function as men in a broader sense in the Christian community and forced the hierarchy to seek some solution to what was an unparalleled problem in the antique tradition.

The first problem faced by these women and the men who observed them was formulating a workable definition of virginity. Gradually, the notion of virginity came to subsume all sorts of women who lived without sexual expression. It became a profession, not a physiological accident; it became a continuing way of life, not an ephemeral characteristic of adolescence. In the last century the Montanist prophetesses, Priscilla and Maximilla, had claimed to be virgins pursuing "manly" careers as wandering preachers, while their critics had maintained that they were simply run-away wives.[1] But as it gradually became the custom to consecrate virgins with quasi-sacramental vows of eternal chastity, people became accustomed to thinking of women as "becoming virgins" at some specific point of decision.[2] Moreover, the condition of virginity had come to transcend the fragile and vulnerable flesh. By the third century, it was accepted as a condition of the soul, which, like marriage, depended on the consent of the practitioner. Even violation could not deprive the sincere devotée of her virginity. Traditions of virgin martyrs defying imperial efforts to sully their purity gave shape to this ideal.[3] Origen's pupil, Gregory Thaumaturge, proclaimed that the women of his diocese in Asia Minor who had been raped by barbarians in the early third century still retained their innocence because they had never yielded their consent to the act.[4]

This definition of virginity as resting on purity in intent rather than simple physical integrity partially opened the ranks of its professors to widows and married women who eschewed the conjugal bed. Thus the concept of virginity loosely came to mean the celibate who followed a particular way of life. It drew in part upon the old order of widowhood for validation, while placing the widows into a larger communal setting.

Tertullian said that the African churches were afire with the question of whether or not virgins were still women.[5] This was clearly no small or trivial question: if they were, the social structure would require reconstruction; if they were not, persons of the female sex would have to be admitted to the rank of men. Either way, recognition of their existence, which was now inescapable, meant that things could never be quite the same again.

The practical implications of the question arose over matters of dress. Tertullian apparently never had to bear the shock of seeing women who actually dressed as men, though this occurred toward the end of the century with increasing frequency. The refusal of some virgins in his day to dress as became women was enough to shake his vision of the natural order. He addressed a sarcastic and horrified tract to the women of his church who claimed that Paul's command that women wear veils while praying in church was not intended for virgins. Tertullian retorted that Paul had used the word "woman" to describe Eve when she was still a virgin; that "woman" meant all females as "man" meant all males. He asked if the recalcitrant virgins would apply their perverse logic to requiring male virgins to veil themselves.[6]

The problem sounds to the modern reader rather like an exercise in absurdity, but to Tertullian it was deadly serious:

> Will you be more modest in public than in church? If your self-devotion is a grace of God and you have received it, 'Why do you boast,' saith He, 'As if you have not received it?' Why by your ostentation of yourself, do you judge others? Is it that, by your boasting, you invite others unto good? Nay, but even you

> yourselves run the risk of losing, if you boast; and you drive
> others unto the same perils! What is assumed from love of
> boasting, is easily destroyed.[7]

Clearly, the problem which would beset the clergy for centuries had
now arisen. The virgins would not be silent and submissive. They
boasted about their superiority, they advertised their state by dress-
ing in an eccentric manner. They behaved as though they had the
dignity of men. In yet another tract, Tertullian returned to the problem, citing an incident he had witnessed himself:

> I know plainly that in a certain place a virgin of less than twen-
> ty years of age was placed in the order of widows! If the bishop
> had been bound to accord her any relief, he might, of course,
> have done it in some other way without detriment to the
> respect due to discipline, that such a miracle, not to say
> monster, should not be pointed at in the church, a virgin-
> widow![8]

Even more appalling was the fact that the monster did not veil her
head as widows did.

We could dismiss Tertullian as a simple misogynist if he always
carried on in this hostile and forbidding tone. But he did not. Despite
his defense of Christian marriage, he was increasingly drawn
toward the ascetic movement and was personally close to some of its
female practitioners. He called them his "best beloved sisters,"[9]
and "handmaids of the living God, my fellow servants and sisters."[10] Even his famous display of bad temper, in which he urged
women to veil themselves because "you are the devil's gateway,"
was quickly modified by the explanation that their ornaments came
from evil agencies. "For you, too, (women as you are) have the
self-same angelic nature promised as your reward, the self-same sex
as men: the self-same advancement to the dignity of judging does the
Lord promise you."[11] And in the second book, he stressed the idea
that men also must cast out vanity and embrace a single standard of
behavior.[12]

In a sense then, Tertullian was not inclined to reject altogether the
idea that in some mystical manner virgins were indeed manly. He
went further than his orthodox contemporaries when, in the end, he
accepted the implicit denigration of marriage and procreation
embedded in the virginal ideal. But what were the practical implica-

tions of granting female virgins an allegorical manhood? Should these virile women live as men might live? Should they be allowed to carry out the functions of men in the church? Or should they be set apart in some way in an order of their own? In the latter case, might they not seem to occupy a superior position in a hierarchy of spiritual achievement which opposed the administrative ranks of the clergy? Tertullian was still speaking in an orthodox voice when he demurred against giving virgins even the responsibility for teaching and counselling women which had traditionally been reserved for deaconesses. We have already seen that, at that time, the church was inclined to see the female diaconate as an appropriate position for virgins and consecrated widows (as a means of closing it to clerical wives.)[13] But Tertullian argued that only true widows "who have travelled down the whole course of probation whereby a female can be tested," should take up the task. Clearly, he believed the training of women should reinforce traditional gender roles rather than prepare women for a fuller share of religious responsibilities. "So true is this, that on the ground of her position, nothing in the way of public honor can be permitted to a virgin."[14]

There is no real mystery in this champion of asceticism's desire to deny public positions to virgins. He feared that they might grasp at the sacramental roles increasingly monopolized by the male clergy. He fiercely opposed the women who considered Thecla a role model and claimed the right to baptize by her example.[15] He saw their refusal to veil themselves as an effort to claim some prerogative that was men's alone:

> It is not permitted to a woman to speak in the church, nor to teach, nor to baptize, nor to offer, nor to claim for herself a lot in any manly function, not to say sacerdotal office. Let us inquire if any of these be lawful to a virgin?[16]

Naturally, the answer was no. It was not a frivolous puritanism that compelled Tertullian to reiterate so obsessively that a virgin is still a woman, subject to the disciplines that characterize women; to attempt so fiercely to deny any mark of distinction or glory to the consecrated women of his community. He would have been a happier man if the women he knew would hide behind their veils. But it is clear that they would not.

This study is not concerned with the sentiments of the Fathers, but rather with the acts and opinions of women that must have provoked their censures. Thus, Tertullian's repeated admonitions to Christian virgins seem to point to a community which was neither heretical nor as submissive as he and other clergymen thought they should be. It takes no strenuous leap of the imagination to conjecture that women who demonstrated regularly that they were prepared to die for their faith in the public arena felt that they also had a right to live for it fully. Already, legends were circulating of heroic Christian women who, like Pelagia, were living manly lives disguised as men.[17]

Some consecrated women apparently felt that, having transcended their sexuality, they could undertake radically innovative life-styles. Widespread testimony indicates that many consecrated women, singly or in groups, had set up housekeeping with men who were neither their husbands nor their blood relatives. Often, indeed, they were sympathetic clergymen, probably drawn from the ranks of those who were convinced of the superiority of celibacy to marriage and were, therefore, likely to find themselves in sympathy with the struggles of ascetic women to redefine their own lives. As a Montanist, Tertullian had no hesitation in criticizing these joint households found among the orthodox clergy.[18] However, he came to believe that his Montanist brethren should embrace them as a preferable solution to the practical problems that might lead them into "digamy."

> Your pretexts (for a second marriage) are: the necessities of props to lean on; a house to be managed; a family to be governed; chests and keys to be guarded; the wool-spinning to be dispensed; food to be attended to; cares to be generally lessened. . . . Then take some spiritual wife. Take to yourself from among the widows one fair in faith, dowered with poverty, sealed with age. You will thus make a good marriage. A plurality of such wives is pleasing to God.[19]

Not everyone heeded the requirements of age and poverty, however. The presence of *virgines subintroductae* in the houses of clergymen became the subject of repeated scandals and called forth rebukes from the Fathers of the third and early fourth centuries. The most famous of these incidents involved Paul of Samosata, Bishop of Palmyra, whose clergy complained about him to the Bishops of Rome and finally appealed to the Emperor Aurelian for aid. In 268, they charged that he had abused his office and made considerable money from it; he had encouraged his followers to regard him as an angel and trained a choir of women to sing psalms in his honor:

> And, as to the *subintroductae* as the Antiochenes call them, his own and those of the presbyters and deacons in his company, with whom he joins in concealing both this and other incurable sins (though he knows of, and has convicted them), that he may have them under obligation to him, and that they may not dare through fear for themselves to accuse him of his misdemeanours in word and deed; yea, he had even made them rich, for which cause he is the beloved and admired of those who affect such conduct—but why should we write of such things? But we know, beloved, that the bishop and the priesthood as a whole should be a pattern to the people of all good works; and we are not ignorant of this; how many have fallen through procuring *subintroductae* for themselves, while others are under suspicion; so that even if it be granted that he does nothing licentious, yet he ought at least to guard against the suspicion that arises from such a practice, lest he cause someone to stumble and induce others also to imitate him. For how could he rebuke another, or counsel against a slip, as it is written, seeing that he had sent one away already and has two in his company in the flower of youth and beauty and even if he goes away somewhere, he brings them around with him, living all the while in luxury and surfeit.[20]

Although the case of Paul of Samosata was a notorious case and the clergy who wrote this letter against him had many more grave charges to lay against him, the letter seems to indicate that the practice of keeping *subintroductae* in clerical establishments was widespread, at least in Syria. In Carthage, in the middle of the third century, Cyprian advised one of his suffragans to excommunicate those virgins who claimed to have remained intact, though habitually sleeping in the same bed with their "brothers," one of whom was a deacon.[21] The bishop advised that virgins should not be allowed to share a house, never mind a bed, with any man because of the scandal:

> Let no one think that she can be defended by this excuse, that she can be examined and proved whether she is a virgin since both the hands and the eyes of midwives are often deceived so

that, even though she may have been found an incorrupt virgin in that part where a woman can be, she may yet have sinned in some other part of the body which can be corrupted and yet cannot be examined. How great a confession of infamy and of reproach assuredly, are the very acts of sleeping together in the same bed, the very embracing, the very conversing, and the kissing, and the scandalous and disgraceful sleeping of two lying together.[22]

In the end, the deacon was excommunicated and the virgins who were found to be intact were restored to communion, but could not return to their male cohabitors. In other cases, where a greater degree of decorum was preserved, we lack sufficient evidence to examine the lives of virgins in great detail. But, plainly, these women were sometimes at a loss to formulate a manner of life suitable to the celibate woman. Some must have lived independently, and others probably pooled their resources to live together. The *subintroductae* can never have been numerous, but they may have been a particularly adventurous fraction of the virginal community who sought boldly to alter their condition by living like men among men. They did not surrender easily. As late as the sixth century, Justinian was still legislating to control the practice in the east, while Gregory the Great exposed its dangers in Italy.

It may seem ill-advised to us, and even singularly pointless, to escape marriage only to engage in a chaste cohabitation. It seems almost inevitable that the *subintroductae* would have found themselves once more in the coils of traditional gender roles without the accompanying privileges accorded to a Roman matron. But to the virgins themselves it may have seemed a brave experiment in a new liberty; an assault on the increasingly male citadel of the clergy where they could hope, unofficially at least, to share in some of the spiritual duties and experiences from which they had been barred by reason of their gender. As the companions and helpers of priests and bishops, they could at least expect a field for the exercise of that unofficial, manipulative power which usually has been accorded to women.

While the clergy sought to integrate these women into the Christian community, they had no intention of surrendering any portion of its own position. Nor did they intend to institutionalize a life-style which depended on claims of transcendence and admitted of no concrete check. Patristic writers had stretched the definition of virginity to make it a spiritual condition common to an "order" of celibate women. However, as Cyprian understood, the process worked two ways: if virginity were a state of mind and virgins an "order," then virgins were subject to a set of behavioral regulations which would provide material reflection of their spiritual condition.

The Veiling of Virgins

If virginity were a state of mind which might, with qualifications, be attained by chaste widows and rebellious wives, it followed, in the opinion of the Fathers, that it might be lost by engaging in behavior unbecoming to a virgin. Thus, they began to delineate conditions for recognizing "true virgins," which would circumscribe and define the place they would occupy in the church. At the same time, the virgins and their champions began to develop an ideology that equated sexual purity with the apex of spiritual perfection. Both attitudes were expressed by the compilers of the *Apostolic Constitutions*, who commended women who had the gift of virginity and, for the first time in patristic writing, gave them official encouragement. At the same time, they reminded their readers that Jesus had not commanded or even recommended virginity in the New Testament, and even Paul had explicitly denied that his advice on the subject came from the Lord. Recognizing that the gift was not for all, the compilers tried to take steps to prevent those who had it from believing that they were superior to their married co-religionists. Particularly, they warned that the woman who undertook to live the virgin life must express her physical integrity through works reflective of a chaste spirit:

> Let her not be gadding about, nor rambling unseasonably; not double-minded, but grave, continent, sober, pure, avoiding the conversation of many and especially of those who are of ill repute.[23]

Women who wished to live outside the authority of husbands, therefore, were to be inhibited, if that proved possible, from living the busy lives of those whom Clement had seen in Alexandria. Virgins who wished to form a separate stratum in the Christian social hierarchy were to be subject to special standards of decorum in exchange for institutional recognition. A way of life suitable to "true virgins" was therefore formulated.

Third-century writers focused on questions of suitable dress. Clement of Alexandria had argued that sober and modest clothing,
faithful to the lineaments of nature, and faces unmarred by cosmetics were suitable to married as well as unmarried women. Tertullian and his successors, however, were more distracted by the
problem of virgins who followed the styles of their married sisters.
They demanded that virgins aggressively obliterate any attractions
they might have for men. In fact, Tertullian constructed an argument for the social control of women still heard in many modern
circles.

In a treatise, *On the Apparel of Women,* Tertullian articulated
what was clearly half of a dialogue on the question of temptation.
Apparently, women had objected to efforts to reform their dress.
They had said that, being devoted to chastity, they should be allowed to enjoy the beauty of clothing and jewelry for its own sake.
They disclaimed all responsibility for the yearnings that lustful men
might suffer at the sight of them. They maintained that they had not
set out to tempt anyone and could not be responsible for the
weakness of those who saw them. Tertullian rebuked them and
warned that they would share in the sins they provoked in men.[24] In
still another work on the same theme, he even threatened them with
the retaliatory violence of men whose lust might be rendered uncon-
trollable by their display of beauty.[25]

Tertullian's position was not new in the third century and it is not
yet outdated.[26] In the third century, however, it played a vital role in
taming and constraining the claims of virile women to equality
beyond the strictly spiritual. The dour prescriptions of Tertullian
probably represented only one end of a spectrum of male voices
raised in response to self-assertive virgins. More moderate
clergymen probably found it politic to address the females in their
own congregations in somewhat milder tones, particularly where
the women in question were rich and powerful enough to enjoy lux-
urious wardrobes, expensive jewelry, and the services of hair-
dressers and other beauticians. But they did not wholly reject the
fierce puritanism of Tertullian in these matters. The adherents of orthodoxy continued to preserve his voice even after he had been lost
to heresy. Unlike other heterodox teachers, he clearly offered them
something that they valued very much.

A generation or so after Tertullian, Cyprian of Carthage was still
addressing the uncontrolled and somewhat impudent virgins
flourishing in the African church. Obviously, he felt they still need-

ed to be told to dress and live like virgins. Probably he had no more success than Tertullian in forcing them to give up their jewelry, cosmetics and wealthy appurtenances in favor of modesty and charitable works.[27] They continued to give lavish parties and even to attend weddings, where they were regularly seen participating in the bawdy jokes and horseplay that normally accompanied those events.[28] Cyprian urged the virgins of his diocese to desist from going to the baths and flaunting their bodies about among men at the fashionable morning hours.[29]

If the virgins regarded these tracts as insulting, they neither allowed them to enforce a change in their manner of living nor to drive them from communion with the congregation. Unfortunately, we do not have a record of both sides of the dispute. Later churchmen preserved the tracts and letters of the Fathers that conformed to their own precepts, but these are by no means the only ones that were written. Perhaps some of these women even wrote public defenses of their open way of living. In any case, the clergy's repeated admonitions amply demonstrate that their desire to limit the virgins to lives of inconspicuous self-abnegation was frequently frustrated.

Yet these same busy virgins represented a life that was increasingly viewed as the highest model of practical Christianity. During this period, efforts to impose celibacy on the clergy multiplied. At the beginning of the fourth century, clerical celibacy was even briefly introduced into church law by the bishops gathered in council at Elvira in Spain.[20] Though the effort was annulled by the Council of Nicaea a few years later, it did not prohibit male virgins or chaste widows from becoming clergymen. The *Apostolic Constitutions,* on the other side, reiterated the Pauline mold as the norm.[31]

The writings of the proponents of male celibacy in the pre-Constantinian church generally have not been preserved, so we have little direct information about their motives. It is possible that the desire to impose celibacy on the clergy resulted from the generalized misogyny evident in some gnostic literature, just as it appears probable that hostility to men was one of the appealing elements of the asexual life for women. There is no question, however, that by the middle of the third century the renunciation of sex was viewed by many as the highest act of love and sacrifice that a Christian could make for the sake of Jesus. Virginity readily came to symbolize a moral integrity and spiritual purity, far beyond that of the married clergy.

The confrontation of the ascetic and the clerical ideals was dramatically illustrated by the difficulties of Origen. When he was first teaching in Alexandria as Clement's successor, he clashed more than once with the bishop, who was only beginning to assert his authority in the city.[32] Indeed, the bishop's ability to control Origen, who was famous for his virtue as well as for his learning, became the supreme test of his authority. A temporary resolution was achieved when Bishop Demetrius took Origen and his school directly under his protection and exercised his priestly power to absolve Origen of the sin of auto-castration. But when Demetrius attempted to control lay preaching in the city and subject Origen to his approval, the great philosopher left the city and the bishop lost control of his following.

This was the first of many clashes between the competing ascetic and clerical elites which mark the history of the church. Throughout the third century, the married clergy sought to impose their authority on diverse groups of ascetics who represented the older tradition of direct communion with one another and with God. By and large, they were successful. By the middle of the century, when the Emperor Decius renewed the effort to extirpate the Christian religion from his Empire, he directed his threats against the bishops, believing that if he could wipe them out, their flocks would swiftly fall away.

To be sure, this organized clergy provided courageous leadership for their beleaguered communities. They controlled the teaching and preaching, organized the support systems upon which the Christian poor depended, and legislated morality and orthodoxy for their flocks. Yet, with all this, they came out second in the competition of virtue. The genuine ascetic was increasingly viewed as an intrinsically greater being, and female virgins were the most common representatives of the species.

Even though our direct sources are limited to the clerical literature aimed at enhancing their own control, they make it clear that ascetic women were winning the struggle to make a place for themselves in the developing community. They were women who had the power to choose other alternatives; the commands of bishops and the scolding of moralists could not constrain them. These third-century virgins who would not veil themselves and would not refrain from living openly among the laity were inventing their own lives; they were not being bullied or forced into anything.

In the first two Christian centuries, as we have seen, no single authoritative document encouraged women to reject the traditional life of marriage and childbearing. Even Paul had addressed himself primarily to men in answering the questions regarding celibacy forwarded by Chloe from Corinth.

The gnostics, who urged everyone to reject the tyranny of the flesh, were uncompromisingly cut off from the church. No Father of this period celebrated the ideal of women living free from men.[33]

Paul was suspicious of women who wished to remain alone and his successors reiterated his age restrictions for "true" widows with depressing regularity. Generally, the Fathers expected widows to marry again, though they did not attempt to force them into it with the strictures of Roman Law. Tertullian was completely out of line with orthodox thought when he mounted his violent campaign against "digamy." But by the third century, the number of women of all ages living alone had multiplied, and the widows gradually tended to be submerged into the company of virgins.[34] Moreover, most of the writers of that period tacitly conceded that virgins, as a group, *were* women. Though Cyprian of Carthage once suggested that his readers might tend to think of virgins as men, his tract, like other literature on virginity, was clearly addressed to women.[35]

If the Fathers did not write on the subject of an order of virgins; if they did not even recognize it until the virgins had already emerged as a group who could not be ignored, then clearly the notion could only have been formulated by its practitioners. They were attempting to foist their own values on the Christian community. The church was not attempting to cut away its female membership from the ancient values governing marriage and childbearing. It was attempting, in fact, to strengthen some of those values by championing the idea of marriage based on mutual interests and mutual consent rather than on the political and economic interests of the families of the respective partners. The church's prohibition of divorce and its opposition to child-exposure were all aimed at the creation of a strong nuclear family to which individual caprice would be subordinate though individual commitments to God would continue to justify defiance of both imperial and familial authority.

The church recognized the order slowly and almost unwillingly. Its contribution to the formulation of the virginal ideal was generally negative in that it sought to restrict its practitioners from entering into a wider sphere of activity. Thus, the compilers of the *Apostolic Constitutions* were still willing to bestow the female diaconate on virgins and widows but, by the third century, they severely restricted its scope. The transition is apparent in the document itself. An early canon retained the idea that deaconesses are necessary for the baptism of female catechumens.[36] But in a later canon, this was firmly refuted. "Women are not to baptize . . . for it is against nature for women to perform a priestly role."[37] Furthermore, if any woman made the claim that she was exceptional, the compilers recalled Mary Magdalene, Salome, the Virgin Mary, and others of Jesus' companions: "We do not permit women to teach, for Christ did not include women among the twelve though eligible women were there."[38]

We are so accustomed to this stance that it may come as a shock to realize that it was introduced so late into the canons of the church. The first-century Fathers had prohibited women from performing the eucharistic service, but they had certainly not made any effort to prevent them from teaching. Throughout the second century, women did teach, and Clement of Alexandria cited the need for women teachers as one of his arguments in defence of clerical marriage.

Thus, an order of women outside of marriage was being founded and gradually incorporated into the Christian social hierarchy. The compilers of *The Apostolic Constitutions* outlined a liturgy for the ceremonial consecration of virgins and widows in the church. With some anxiety, they stressed that under no circumstances should anyone construe the ceremony as an ordination or confuse its recipients, in any way, with the clergy.[39]

Brides of Christ

It was with some timorous misgivings, therefore, that the leaders of the church finally gave recognition to a new social order of unmarried women. Their admiration for the virgin's devotion to a life of purity was bounded by their reluctance to bestow even the faintest suggestion of a sacerdotal status upon her. If women dedicated to a life without womanly functions believed that they could eliminate the barriers between male and female, or surmount them to become "men" in practice, they were informed that the transformation would be completed only in heaven. Indeed, Tertullian threatened that they would lose their claim to superior virtue by their effrontery:

Arabia's heathen females will be your judges, who cover not

only the head but the face also, so entirely that they are content with one eye free, to enjoy rather half the light than to prostitute the entire face.[40]

Veiling was the sign of women's subjection, he plainly said, and all women must assume it.

But to whom were virgins subject? Searching for an answer, Tertullian triumphantly turned back to the idea of the eschatalogical family, an idea embedded in the New Testament, and steadily elaborated over the centuries. Christians habitually called God their father and, by the second century, they had begun to call the church their mother. They called one another brother and sister. It was not, therefore, a giant step for Tertullian to add conjugal imagery to the scheme:

> Be veiled, virgin, if virgin you are! for you ought to blush. If you are a virgin, shrink from the gaze of many eyes. Let no one wonder at your face; let no one perceive your falsehood. You do well in falsely assuming the married character if you veil your head. Nay, you do not assume it falsely, for you are wedded to Christ. To him, you have surrendered your body. Act as becomes your husband's discipline.[41]

Almost by accident, judging from the off-handed tone of the passage, Tertullian had stumbled on what the clergy would come to regard as a perfect solution to the dilemma. With the defeat of their prophetic competitors, the third-century clergy generally regarded themselves as the representatives on earth of Christ. Thus, they could claim vicarious authority over his brides. In some ways, indeed, this direct relationship between the representatives of the church and the unmarried Christian woman conformed more comfortably to the individualistic tendencies of the faith than did the interpolation of a husband between the woman and the priest. The idea of the virgin as the bride of Christ suggested a way of defining her position that freed the clergy to praise and admire her without fearing her competition.

Not all women accepted these conditions. Many dropped away from this church into Montanist sects which still revered prophecy or into other heretical groups; some devoted themselves to other deities. In the fourth century, Ephiphanius of Cyprus encountered gnostic women who instructed him in the mysteries of their doctrine. Still others, he maintained, had been advancing their ideas in the Egyptian church while masquerading as orthodox.[42] Unfortunately we have no other information regarding these dissenting Christians, who were rooted out by their bishops. However, the gnostic books which advanced the idea that the flesh was evil and procreation a work of the devil were collected and preserved in the famous Nag Hammadi library. Modern archeologists found them there, not far from the site of the first known monastic community in the Egyptian desert, founded by Pachomius late in the third century.[43]

The virgins known to Tertullian, Cyprian, and other third-century fathers were not gnostics, however. They remained within the orthodox church where they had at least gained recognition for a way of life that freed them from the constraints of marriage and opened the way to experiments with new roles. They did not succeed in actually turning themselves into functional men, as far as the clergy were concerned. However, the history of asceticism during the next two or three centuries was marked by new attempts to redefine gender roles.

However negatively, conciliar legislation for several centuries recognized the existence of these efforts. The Council of Nîmes condemned women for presuming to claim admission to the diaconate.[44] The Council of Carthage forbade them to be ordained as presbyters.[45] The first Council of Nicaea condemned deaconesses who wore habits suggesting that they were clergy.[46] At the end of the fourth century, one council is said to have recognized the ministerial function of women in teaching and baptizing other women, as did Epiphanius, though he prohibited any effort to extend their sacerdotal function.[47]

There seems almost to be a direct relationship between the success of the clergy in defining the virgin within the spectrum of womanliness and their willingness to praise the state as one of superior virtue. Late in the third century, Methodius produced the first piece of orthodox Christian literature devoted to the praise of virginity as the highest manifestation of the Christian life. In a rather stilted and self-conscious effort to emulate Plato, he presented his arguments in the form of a *Symposium of Ten Virgins*. These women had overcome the difficulties of a long and dangerous road to gather in the garden of Arete (Virtue), daughter of Philosophy, for supper and an evening of intellectual discourse. Their hostess greeted them, elegantly but simply dressed and innocent of all cosmetics, inviting them to enter and prepare to present their reflections on the virgin life.[48] The work is dedicated to the proposition that virginity is the highest stage of human achievement. In the first discourse, "Marcella" explains that it emerged so late in history because human social life had to evolve toward perfection, just as babies evolve to maturity. As the nearest condition to celestial perfection attainable on earth, virginity could have no practitioners until the limits of family life had first been explored. Finally, however, the virgins emerged as a chosen elite, singled out from among the multitudes of the saved to stand singing a new song before the Lord.[49]

This reflects a spiritual ordering which Tertullian himself had come to recognize toward the end of his life. Defining chastity as the renunciation of sexuality, he distinguished three kinds of virgins: virgins from birth, virgins from baptism, and virgins who eschewed the marital bed:

> The first species is virginity from one's birth; the second, virginity from one's second birth, that is, from the font, which keeps pure in the marriage state by mutual compact or else perseveres in widowhood from choice. A third grade remains monogamy when, after the interception of a marriage once contracted, there is thereafter a renunciation of sexual connection. The first virginity is of happiness, total ignorance of that from which you will afterwards wish to be freed; the second of virtue, condemning that power which you know full well; the third. . .is the glory of moderation. . .not regretting a thing which has been taken away.[50]

This ranking was recognized institutionally in the order of entering and attending services laid out in the *Apostolic Constitutions*. The entire community was grouped according to gender and position, with the virgins and widows in the lead.[51] Like his master, Origen, Gregory Thaumaturge placed virgins next to the angels in the celestial hierarchy:

> True virginity has a kind of affinity and equality with the angels. . . .All who have preserved the lamp of virginity unextinguished shall be privileged to receive the amarinthine crown of immortality.[52]

For all his misgivings about the behavior of individual virgins in Carthage, Cyprian acclaimed the group as "the flower of the tree that is the Church, the beauty and adornment of spiritual grace, the image of God reflecting the holiness of the Lord, the most illustrious part of Christ's flock."[53]

In this acceptance of the ideology of virginity, the church was moving dangerously close to the heresies of the second century which their foremost theologians had expended so much effort to suppress. Third-century churchmen had brought a difficult and dangerous element into the well-ordered social structure they had inherited from their predecessors. There appears, at first glance, to be very little reason why a married clergy should have opened their church so completely to the pretensions of unmarried women or why they were willing to embrace a radical vision that so implicitly denigrated marriage and procreation. We can only conclude that it was the price of a settlement with a portion of their membership numerous enough and influential enough to be worth such large concessions. The virgins, the widows, and their supporters imposed their ideology on the church as the price of their adherence to it.

The thin line between orthodox ideals of chastity and a heretical rejection of the flesh was all too vividly illustrated in the career of Tertullian. At length, he came to condemn marriage as "nothing but nuptial and dotal contracts which, mayhap, distinguish it from adultery and fornication."[54] Orthodox admirers of virginity saw from the first that their position was full of risks. Methodius devoted his second panegyric to "Theophilia's" argument that the clear superiority of virginity must never be taken to imply that marriage and procreation were unacceptable to Christian morality. Like Paul, centuries earlier, he was concerned to assert the proposition that it is not a sin to marry.[55]

The age of prophets and wandering evangelists was over. The separation of women within the church had ended, and the clergy had taken over their old mission of teaching and even baptizing female catechumens. As brides of Christ, they were to hold an honored but circumscribed place. But there had been a dialogue, a major confrontation in the age-old battle of the sexes. The continued presence of this class of women within the Christian church was ensured only by clerical recognition of their special place.

But there were virgins before there were patristic proponents of virginity. There were whole communities of consecrated women before the fathers of the church found a place for them in the larger structure. By the middle of the third century, they had been categorized and satisfactorily labelled. At last, it became possible to admire them and even to maintain that through Christianity the human race had finally evolved to a stage of social development heretofore unattainable:

> But when the earth had become populated from end to end . . . , God did not suffer mankind to remain in the old ways. He took thought how men might make progress and advance further on the road to heaven, . . . that first they were to advance from brother-sister unions to marrying wives from other families; then they were to give up practicing multiple marriage like brute beasts, as though born for mere intercourse. The next step was to take them from adultery; and next to advance them to continence and from continence to virginity when they trained themselves to despise the flesh and come to anchor unafraid in the peaceful haven of immortality.[56]

Conclusion

The strictly patterned structures of ancient society were already in a state of disrepair when Jesus preached. The Roman Empire had completed the political absorption of all the older states of the Mediterranean world and the process of reducing its cultural variety to a uniform Hellenism was already far advanced. At the same time, the old family-centered society of Rome was being drastically eroded by the individualism which sprang from this hectic cosmopolitanism. During the first three centuries during which Christianity spread through the body of this Empire, the Romans strove incessantly to shore up the antique family with coercive legislation. It was a doomed effort. One of the earliest pieces of Christian legislation issued by Constantine in the fourth century was the abrogation of the Augustan marriage laws and the extension of the right of three children to celibate women.

This legislation represented a profound change in the social structure in that it admitted women into full legal personhood without the intervening authority of a father or husband to control her public life. These celibate women represented an unknown social species. They followed a road no one had yet charted. I have tried to show that it was a road taken on their own initiative, without the guidance of men. In the course of this work, I have been asked whether they might have been acting out of an internalized misogyny that caused them to fear and hate their own sexuality. For some of them, this may certainly have been the case, but I see no particular reason to believe that it was very often the primary reason why this group of women fought so hard to free themselves from subordination to the interests of families and the men who ruled families.

We are talking about only a few women. Most women, even among the Christians, married and bore children. They had their own reasons for believing in Christ and cleaving to his church. Even among the celibate, the free, unmarried life cannot have been the only attraction of the new religion. Nor did celibacy recommend itself only to women. Sources on male virgins are even scarcer than those that relate to females, but from the first century on they do exist. Pagan as well as Christian men very often avoided marriage, though in many cases, they did not avoid sexual connections as well. Whether or not they did so, the experiences of unmarried men can have had very little in common with those of unmarried women. Men had always enjoyed a wide sphere of public life beyond the confines of their families and, as celibates, they could continue to do so undisturbed.

Celibacy, however, was almost incompatible with the definition of woman, particularly asexual celibacy. I have attempted to discuss how that changed both in the social vision of Christian writers and in the social reality that emerged in third-century Christian communities. Early Christians were loosely organized over a wide area; congregations were left largely on their own to formulate the terms of their lives with the Gospels for their guides. Some women interpreted the message of Jesus as a commandment to turn away from the traditional demands of family life. With only fragments of teaching from the New Testament and the inspiration of the women who appear in its pages, they rejected the filial obedience, conjugal subjection, and maternal cares, which constituted the only acceptable rule of life for women in the ancient world. They set themselves to reconstruct the social woman apart from her relationship to the patriarchal family.

Ancient laws did not recognize the existence of unmarried women except to keep them from unruly behavior. Even the Vestal Virgins were tightly controlled and eventually expected to retire into marriage. Widows were ordered by law to remarry as swiftly as possible. Other unmarried women were simply swept into the darkness of the marginal, unrecognized non-entities for whom the social system had no place.

But Christians welcomed the new individualism and built the foundations of their faith on the fragments of the old structures. Jesus insisted that the marginal people, the humble, the obscure, the "last," would come first in his kingdom. Among these were certainly unmarried women.

Though they had no recognized identity among contemporary social observers, the world of Jesus was full of unattached women who performed many functions and sometimes even enjoyed wealth. Many of these women accepted the new faith and spread it enthusiastically. Sometimes they died for it. In asking how and why they chose to live in it, we must assume that there were powerful attractions. I have based this work on the idea that one of them was the opportunity to redefine their own identities and to validate their man-free condition.

I have tried to depict these women as heroines of their own lives, as the active pioneers of the Christian life rather than its passive subjects. I have tried to show how the renunciation of sexuality can represent liberation and a new beginning for women who could not or would not find a satisfactory niche in the traditional system. Assuredly, this female vanguard did not gain the field completely. At no point did they succeed in making themselves genuinely equal to men, except on the field of martyrdom and, perhaps, in the heaven that followed. Perpetua's idea that she was becoming a man was not, however, lost. It would recur in the literature of the larger and freer world that the celibate women of the fourth and fifth century occupied and would find many active proponents determined to experiment with a host of new opportunities. Before that could happen, however, the women who debated the qualities and characteristics of virginity in Arete's garden would be faced with the ordeal of Diocletian's persecution, which claimed the lives of a multitude of virgins destined to live in song and story.

We cannot even begin to imagine what it must have been like for men in those times to contemplate women who claimed a place in the social structure for the unmarried and purposefully barren. How did they react to the claims of virgins that they were a superior species, just because they were free of men? As the panelists of the Symposium declared, virginity was the "great vow above all vows."[1] In Heaven, virgins would take precedence over all others except Christ himself and his allegorical bride (Mother Church).[2]

Christianity was swiftly approaching that time when it would become the dominant religion in the ancient Empire and the cultural matrix for the nascent culture of the north. The problem of the claims of virgins and the place of consecrated unmarried women in the triumphant church was to preoccupy many of the Christian leaders of the next two centuries. But that is a different book. For now, we can leave the celibate women of the third century in the garden of virtue. No longer hidden in the penumbra of the patriarchal family, they saw themselves shining and glittering, in the very first ranks of the elect. So they rose at Thecla's signal, joining hands to sing the song they would sing when they led the Christian people to the pinnacles of Heaven itself:

Fleeing from the sorrowful happiness of mortals,
    having despised the luxurious delights of life and love,
We leave marriage and the beds of mortals and a golden
    home for Thee . . .
Escaping from the innumerable enchanting wiles of the
    serpent,
        the flame of fire and the mortal-destroying assaults of
           the beasts . . .
Singing the new song, now the company of virgins attends
    thee
        towards the high heavens, Oh Queen!
All manifestly crowned with white lilies,
    and bearing in their hands bright lights.[3]

References

Introduction

1. Athanasius, *Life of Antony* 2-3, Nicene and Post Nicene Fathers 4.
2. By the second century, it sometimes appears that many women associated celibacy with Christianity and converted to both at the same time, Ross Kraemer, "The conversion of women to ascetic forms of Christianity," *Signs* 6, (1981):298-307.
3. This is the finely argued theory of Stevan Davies, whose book, *The Revolt of the Widows* (Carbondale, IL, 1980), attempts a full-scale examination of the social world of the apocryphal gospels and their authors. Feminist scholars have made brilliant use of women's fiction as a device for interpreting their own social experience. For example, see Elaine Showalter, *A Literature of Her Own* (Princeton, 1977).
4. This thesis has been carefully explored and explicated by Patricia M. Doyle, "Women and Religion: Psychological and Cultural Implications," in Rosemary Ruether, ed. *Religion and Sexism* (New York, 1974), pp. 15-39.
5. *The Passion of Perpetua and Felicity* (London, 1931).
6. My readers will readily note that I have relied on theoretical frameworks already made classic by Mary Douglas, *Purity and Danger* (New York, 1966) and, of course, Simone de Beauvoir, *The Second Sex* (New York, 1974).

Chapter One

1. Mark 2:15.
2. Matthew 21:31-32.
3. For further background and recent bibliography see E. Mary Smallwood, *Jews Under Roman Rule, Pompey to Diocletian,* Studies in Judaism in Late Antiquity, vol. 20 (Leiden, 1976).
4. John 3:22 treats Judaea as a foreign land and one where the Pharisees were strong. John 4:1 and 5:1 locate "Jews" in Jerusalem and depicts them repeatedly as the persecutors of Jesus, in contrast to the Galileans (5:16-18; 7:1-9 et al.).
5. Matthew 14:21.
6. Luke 10:1.
7. Matthew 9:37-38.
8. John 4:28-42.
9. Since Jewish men were expected to marry before the age of twenty five and before undertaking religious study, Jesus should himself have been married long before he began his preaching mission. The implications of this theory have been ingeniously worked out by William E. Phipps in his controversial book, *Was Jesus Married?* (New York, 1970).
10. I have discussed this question at greater length in my paper, "Wives and Widows in Early Christian Thought," *International Journal of Women's Studies* 2 (1977): 6, 575-92. One of the few rabbinical debates traceable to this period concerned the status of co-wives where incest rules prohibited a marriage between the brother-in-law and one of the women. See Jacob Neusner, *A History of the Mishnaic Law of Women,* Studies in Judaism in Late Antiquity, vol. 33 (Leiden, 1980), p. 184.
11. Ibid.

12. This is certainly the judgment of Salo Baron, *Religious and Social History of the Jews,* vol. 2 (New York, 1952), p. 222.

13. McNamara, "Wives and Widows," p. 577.

14. Baron, p. 226.

15. Neusner, P. 186. Matthew 5:32, Jesus prohibited all divorce except for fornication. See also, I. Abrahams, *Studies in Pharisaism and the Gospels* (New York, 1967), pp. 66-78.

16. Matthew 2:18-21.

17. Neusner, 180.

18. I Timothy 2:12.

19. Philo of Alexandria (Philo Judaeus), *Speculum Legibus* 2. 24, *Works,* ed. and trans. F. H. Colson and G. H. Whitaker, Loeb Classical Library (Cambridge, Mass, 1962).

20. Ibid., 2, 25-48.

21. Luke 1:26-28.

22. Luke 2:36-38.

23. *Speculum Legibus,* 2. 24.

24. See for example, Clement of Rome, "Address to the Greeks," 4-5 (New York, 1947). On the other side, the atmosphere of the Diaspora led to a deterioration of some of the traditional privileges of Jewish women. The Greek practice of submitting a woman to male guardianship in business affairs was gaining favor against the Jewish tradition that a woman's only guardian was her father, Victor Tcherikover, *Hellenistic Civilization and the Jews* (New York, 1959), p. 350.

25. Harry J. Leon, *The Jews of Ancient Rome* (Philadelphia, 1960).

26. Shaye, J. D. Cohen, "Women in the Synagogues of Antiquity," *Conservative Judaism,* vol. 34, 2, pp. 23-29, found the title given to women in inscriptions from Caria, Smyrna, and Crete argues that it reflects the autonomous religious practices of pre-rabbinic communities of the first century.

27. Philo of Alexandria, *De Vita Contemplativo,* 476, 23-24; 481, 22-24; 483, 42; 481, 1, *Works,* Loeb Classical Library (Cambridge, Mass, 1962).

28. Josephus, *Jewish Antiquities,* 15. The same work, 10.4, compares the Essenes with Pythagoreans, but this was probably part of Josephus' agenda for reconciling the Jewish and Hellenistic traditions. Charles Guignebert, *The Jewish World in the Time of Jesus* (New York, 1959), p. 155 argues that their teachings are a logical extension of certain Jewish ideas of the period.

29. *Historia Naturalis,* 5. 16, 4, Loeb Classical Library (Cambridge, Mass, 1963).

30. *Hypothetica, Works,* Loeb Classical Library (Cambridge, Mass, 1962). Leonard Swidler expands on Essene misogyny in *Biblical Affirmations of Women* (Philadelphia, 1979), pp. 51-52.

31. *Jewish War,* 2. 8, 13, Loeb Classical Library (London, 1926).

32. *Apology for the Jews,* fragments preserved in Eusebius, *Praeparatio Evangelica,* 8. 11, *Sources Chrétiennes,* vol. 206 (Paris, 1974).

33. Charles T. Fritsch, *The Qum'ran Community: Its History and Scrolls* (New York, 1956), p. 104.

34. Millar Burrows, *The Dead Sea Scrolls* (New York, 1955), p. 233.

35. J. Leipoldt, *Die Frau in der Antiken Welt und in Urchristentúm* (Leipzig, 1954), p. 116. See also J. Hempel, "Beobachtungen an der 'syrischen' Jesajarolle vom Totem Meer," *Zeitschrift der deutsch morgenländischen Gesellschaft* (1951), pp. 138-73.

36. Fritsch, 116 ff. connects the ideas of the scrolls with those of John the Baptist and John the Evangelist.

37. The question of the authorship of the four Gospels and the related question of their dating have formed the subject of a vast critical literature in our own century. This literature has recently been surveyed and both questions submitted to a revisionist solution which, for the most part, I find convincing. See John A. T. Robinson, *Re-Dating the New Testament* (London, 1976).

38. Eusebius, *Historia Ecclesiastica,* 3. 24-25, *Sources Chrétiennes,* vol. 41 (Paris,

1974) outlines this process. I do not mean to imply that a sinister plot underlay this early Christian effort at scholarship. But I do want to stress that the stories retained in the New Testament were not the only ones transmitted in early Christian preaching.

39. For some of the most recent work on the New Testament and its bibliography, see William R. Farmer, *The Synoptic Problem: A Critical Analysis* (Macon, 1981).

40. Acts 2:14.

41. Most biblical scholars consider the stories of his birth and appearance in the Temple when he was twelve as post-Resurrection constructs to emphasize parallels with ancient prophecies and to shape new christological theories. The role of Mary in the historical life and mission of Jesus has inspired a mountain of literature. Among recent works see Brown et al., *Mary in the New Testament* (Philadelphia and New York, 1978) and John McHugh, *The Mother of Jesus in the New Testament* (Garden City, 1975). Geoffrey Ashe, *The Virgin* (London, 1976) offers a uniquely imaginative and sympathetic reconstruction of Mary's life drawn from the scanty evidence of the Gospels. The story that Jesus was the son of a Roman soldier named Panderus or Pantherus was refuted by Origen, *Contra Celsum*, 1, 32, Ante Nicene Fathers vol. 4 (Grand Rapids, 1976). For a further discussion, see Marina Warner, *Alone of All Her Sex* (London, 1976), p. 35.

42. Matthew 12:46-50; 13:55-57.

43. John 1:14: "And the Word became flesh and dwelt amongst us, full of grace and truth; we have beheld his glory, glory as of the only Son from the Father."

44. John 2:12.

45. Luke 8:19.

46. Mark 3:31.

47. Ibid., and Matthew 12:46-50.

48. This is a concept formulated by Brown et al., p. 119.

49. Mary may have contributed other stories to John's version which do not appear in the three synoptic Gospels. One is the claim that Jesus began his public life when his mother urged him to intervene miraculously to save her friends from embarrassment at a wedding party (John 2:1-11). His acquiescence was somewhat brusque, echoing the impatient responses of the lost child in the Temple recorded by Luke. Thereafter, he embarked on an extensive preaching mission throughout Galilee and possibly in Jerusalem as well (Matthew 4:12-17; Mark 1:14; Luke 4:14-15). Only John 2:13 maintains that he entered Judaea before the final days of his life.

50. John 13:56.

51. Luke 5:38-40.

52. Paul, I Corinthians 9:5 mentions Cephas (Peter) and other apostles who travel with their wives. Clement of Alexandria, *Stromata* 3, 11, 63 describes the martyrdom of Peter's wife as it was told by second century Christians.

53. *The Gospel of Peter* 1, in Montague R. James, *The Apocryphal New Testament* (Oxford, 1972). P. Styger, *Römische Martyrbegrüfte* (Berlin, 1935), vol. 1, p. 168, noted a depiction of her as a saint leading the owner of a tomb, Lady Veneranda, d. 396, to heaven.

54. Matthew 4:22.

55. Matthew 20:20-28.

56. Matthew 27.

57. Luke 13:10.

58. Luke 7:11-17. This was his second such feat. The raising of Lazarus was also achieved in response to the needs of bereaved women.

59. Matthew 15:21-28; Mark 3:25.

60. Matthew 9:18-26; Mark 5:21-43; Luke 8:40-56.

61. *Acts of Pilate*, 12 in James, *Apocryphal New Testament*.

62. This story is unique to John's Gospel, 4:7-43.

63. Matthew 16:13-20; Mark 8:27-33; Luke 9:18-22.

64. The argument that John's Gospel pre-dated the synoptic gospel is very persuasively presented by Robinson, *Re-Dating the New Testament*.

65. Mark 15:40.

66. *Gospel of Thomas*, 61, in J. M. Robinson, *The Nag Hammadi Library* (New York, 1977).

67. *The Gospel of Philip*, in Robinson, *The Nag Hammadi Library* (New York, 1977).

68. John 19:25.

69. Luke 8:1-3; Mark 16:9, a somewhat shaky passage confirming Mary's discovery of the risen Christ which was omitted by many ancient redactors of the Gospel.

70. For modern observations of this phenomenon, see S. Messing, "Group Therapy and Social Status in the Zar Cult of Ethiopia," in John Middleton, *Magic, Witchcraft, and Curing* (Austin, 1967), pp. 285-295. I. M. Lewis, *Ecstatic Religion* (New York, 1971) provides a broader theoretical study. See also Carroll Smith-Rosenberg, "The Hysterical woman," in E. Katz and A. Rapone, *Women's Experience in America* (New Brunswick, 1980).

71. John 8:53, another instance of a story unique to John.

72. John 11:1-44.

73. Luke 10:38.

74. Luke 7:37 does not relate this story to Lazarus' sister. Matthew 26:6 placed the dinner in Bethany in the house of a Pharisee who criticized her generosity. John 12:1-8 unequivocally identifies her as Mary of Bethany.

75. Luke 23:12, who names Joanna with the women who prepared Jesus for burial.

76. Matthew 27:19.

77. John 19:25-26; Luke 23:28; Matthew 27:55; Mark 15:40.

78. Matthew 28:1.

79. Mark 15:40.

80. Luke 24:10.

81. Mark 16:9.

82. Elaine Pagels, *Gnostic Gospels* (New York, 1979), p. 13. For the text, see Robinson, *Nag Hammadi Library*, p. 471.

Chapter Two

1. Acts 1:14.

2. Acts 2:43-47.

3. Luke 2:38.

4. Josephus, *Jewish Antiquities* 27. 2, 4 Loeb Classical Library (London, 1926). For elaboration, see Charles Guignebert, *The Jewish World at the Time of Jesus* (New York, 1959), p. 70.

5. Acts 2:42. These numbers, like most numbers in ancient chronicles, should be taken cautiously to mean, "more than anyone could count."

6. Acts 5:1-11. It may be a measure of the self-conscious egalitarianism of those first days that the author took care to emphasize that Ananias and Sapphira were interviewed separately, committed their deceptions independently of one another, and received equal punishment from God.

7. Acts 3:45.

8. For a broader treatment, see Leonhard Goppelt, *Apostolic and Post-Apostolic Times* (London, 1970), pp. 36 ff.

9. Clement of Rome, *Second Epistle on Virginity* 5 Ante Nicene Christian Library, vol. 14 (Edinburgh, 1869).

10. Luke 15; 3-10; Mark 2:21.

11. I Corinthians 11:5. Paul appears to be making a special distinction in this command that women veil themselves when praying and prophesying. Possibly he did not see this activity as occurring in a church where, in the same letter, he said that women should keep silence: I Corinthians 15:34-36.

12. Revelation 2:20.

13. Jukka Thurén, "Paulus och Gnosticismen," *Svensk Pastoraltidskrift*, vol. 30-31,

pp. 569-73, suggests that the preaching of women had already come to be associated with gnostic heresy, so that Paul saw the silence of women and their willingness to bear children as twin tests of orthodoxy. I am indebted to John E. Halborg for providing me with a translation of this article.

14. Mark 12:38-44.

15. Luke 18:2-8.

16. Luke 13:10-17.

17. For an excellent exposition of some of these problems, see Patricia Martin Doyle, "Women and Religion: Psychological and Cultural Implications," in Rosemary R. Ruether, *Religion and Sexism* (New York, 1974), pp. 15-39.

18. This ancient ideal of womanhood is most powerfully expressed in Proverbs 31:10-31, which praises the good wife.

19. Two disparate examples are advanced by John Bugge, *Virginitas* (The Hague, 1975) for the high middle ages and, for nineteenth-century America, by Barbara Welter, "The Feminization of American Religion," in M. Hartmann and L. Banner, *Clio's Consciousness Raised* (New York, 1974), pp. 137-157.

20. Matthew 19:3-12 constitutes the fullest presentation of Jesus' views on marriage. The only appearances of Genesis 2:24 in the *Babylonian Talmud* are irrelevant to marriage law. I have discussed this question at some length in "Wives and Widows in Early Christian Thought." Gerhard von Rad's *Commentary on Genesis* (Philadelphia, 1961) is uncompromising in pointing up the irrelevance of the sentence to the patrilineal structure of ancient Israel, where a woman left her family to cleave, even in widowhood, to the family of her husband.

21. Matthew 19:9.

22. John 8:1-11 or Luke 21:38. This story early became detached from the manuscript tradition. Biblical scholars generally accept its authenticity but dispute its authorship and placement.

23. Luke 11:27.

24. This is an opinion further elucidated by Evelyn and Frank Stagg, *Woman in the World of Jesus* (Philadelphia, 1978), pp. 106 ff.

25. Matthew 22:23-30.

26. Matthew 8:18; Luke 9:60. The disciples were instructed, "call no man your father" (Matthew 23:11) . . . "Unless born again" (John 3:1-19). In the apocryphal Gospel of Thomas, they were promised not only a father but a mother in heaven as well, *Nag Hammadi Library*, pp. 128-29.

27. Phyllis Bird, "Images of Women in the Old Testament," in Rosemary R. Ruether, *Religion and Sexism* (New York, 1974), pp. 41-88, argues that the Law was addressed only to men who in turn gave laws to women.

28. Matthew 10:34; Mark 13:12; Luke 12:44-53.

29. Mark 19:29; Matthew 10:30; Luke 14:25.

30. Most convincingly, Elizabeth Schüssler Fiorenza, "Word, Spirit and Power: Women in Early Christian Communities," in Rosemary Ruether and Eleanor McLaughlin, *Women of Spirit: Female Leadership in the Jewish and Christian Traditions* (New York, 1979), pp. 30-70.

31. Wayne Meeks, "The Image of the Androgyne," *History of Religions* 13 (1974): 165-208.

32. I Corinthians 9:5.

33. See J. B. Bauer, "Uxores circumducere," *Biblische Zeitschrift* 3 (1959): 94-102; P. de Labriolle, "Le mariage spirituel," *Revue Historique* 137 (1921): 204-225, and J. McNamara, "Chaste Marriage and Clerical Celibacy," in Vern Bullough and James Brundage, *Sexual Practices in the Medieval Church* (Buffalo, 1981), pp. 22-33.

34. I Corinthians 18. The history and family of Priscilla have been ingeniously reconstructed by Ruth Hoppin, *Priscilla: Author of the Epistle to the Hebrews,* (Philadelphia, 1969).

35. Romans 16:3.

36. II Timothy 4:19.

37. Junia's claim to the apostolate has been denied since the fourteenth century. Prior to that, however, no one doubted that she was a woman. Her masculinization appears to have been a typically scholastic solution to a logical difficulty: if no apostle could be a woman, then Junia must have been a man and her name was masculinized to Junias to prove it. Happily, modern feminist scholarship has rescued her and restored her to her original gender. Bernadette Brooten, "Junia . . . Outstanding Among the Apostles," in Leonard and Arlene Swidler, *Women Priests* (New York, 1977), pp. 141-44, advances both philological and onomastic proofs that there is no record of anyone named "Junias" and no logical way that Greek or Roman practices of creating diminutives could result in such a name. In the same collection, Elizabeth Fiorenza gives more general arguments, "The Apostleship of Women," pp. 134-40.

38. I Timothy 3:11.

39. Clement of Alexandria, *Stromata*, 3; R. Gryson, *Origines du célibate ecclésiastiques du première au septième siècle* (Gembloux, 1970) claims that the apostles' wives were deaconesses.

40. I Timothy 3:2-6.

41. *Stromata* 3. 11, 63.

42. Acts 5:1-11.

43. Leonhard Goppelt, *Apostolic and Post-Apostolic Times* (London, 1970), p. 88.

44. I Corinthians 7:14.

45. Acts 13:12.

46. II Timothy 1:5.

47. I Timothy 5:3-16. This letter is one of the disputed entries in the Pauline canon but Acts 16:1 confirms that Timothy was the son of a Jewish woman "who was a believer" and a Greek father.

48. I Timothy 5:9.

49. See Chapter I, p. 14. The concept was elucidated by Raymond Brown et al., *Mary in the New Testament* (Philadelphia, 1978).

50. Acts 6:1.

51. Acts 6:1-7.

52. Acts 9:36-43.

53. Acts 21:8.

54. Eusebius, in his fourth century *Historia Ecclesiastica* 3. 30, noted the belief advanced by Clement of Alexandria (*Stromata* 3. 6, 52) that Philip gave his daughters in marriage. In refutation of Clement's typical pro-marriage stand, Eusebius cited an earlier letter from Polycrates, Bishop of Ephesus, claiming that Philip fell asleep in Hierapolis with "his two daughters who grew old in virginity, and his other daughter who lived in the Holy Spirit and rests at Ephesus," (*Historia Ecclesiastica* 3. 31, 3). He also cited an earlier text from Proclus which claimed that all four were buried in Hierapolis with their father (*Historia Ecclesiastica* 3. 31, 4). Eusebius, therefore, seemed to be able to show that, despite the claim of the pro-marriage advocate Clement in the late second century, the four daughters who prophesied were believed to have lived and died as virgins. This is an opinion borne out by the *Apostolic Constitutions* 8.2, also of the fourth century, which cited a distinguished list of women prophets from both Old and New Testaments, including Philip's four virgin daughters.

55. Acts 16:13-40.

56. Sarah Pomeroy, *Goddesses, Whores, Wives and Slaves*, (New York, 1975), p. 198. Claudius gave them the right of four children (juridical independence) in exchange for investment in the grain market. Similar persons constructed their own funeral monuments and lesser memorials for their slaves.

57. Acts 17:4.

58. Acts 17:12.

59. Acts 17:34.

60. Collossians 17:15.

61. I Corinthians 1:11.

62. Romans 16:1.

63. Clement of Alexandria, true to his pro-marital stance, maintained that the recipient was his wife, *Stromata* 3. 6, 52. The *Oxford Annotated Bible* suggests that "Syzygus" may not have been a description ("true yokemate") but, rather, the proper name of a man.

64. Romans 16:6-12; *Acts of Paul and Thecla,* in James, *Apocryphal New Testament.*

65. A survey of these opinions can be found in Elizabeth Fiorenza, "Word, Spirit, Power . . ." in Ruether and McLaughlin, *Women of Spirit,* p. 62-63, n. 24-28; and in F. R. Crownfield, A Historical Approach to the New Testament (New York, 1960), pp. 248 ff.

66. Fiorenza, "Word, Spirit, Power," p. 37, conjectures that the prohibition against women preaching (II Timothy 3-6) might have been directed against a female rival of Paul's. L. Zscharnack, *Der Dienst der Frau* (Gottingen, 1902), p. 40, sets it in the context of Montanist claims of descent from Ammia of Philadelphia whom Eusebius included among the orthodox prophetesses (*Historia Ecclesiastica* 3. 31, 39).

67. I Corinthians 5:1.

68. I Corinthians 6:9 and 6:16.

69. I Corinthians 7.

70. The long history of successive imperial efforts to enforce the Augustan marriage laws was studied by J. Bouché-Leclercq, "Les lois démographiques d'Auguste," *Revue Historique* 57 (1895): 241-92. I have pursued this question further in "Wives and Widows in Early Christian Thought."

71. I Corinthians 7:10-11.

72. I Corinthians 7:8-11.

73. I Corinthians 7:39-40.

74. I Corinthians 7:25-35. Lucien Legrand, *Biblical Doctrine of Virginity* (New York, 1963), pp. 89 ff. has explored the relationship of this idea to similar sentiments in Epictetus and other Stoic philosophers.

75. The *King James Bible* gives "virgin" as the translation here rendered as "betrothed," following the *Oxford Annotated Bible.* Some editors have construed it to refer to a daughter.

76. See arguments by N. Achelis, *Virgines Subintroductae* (Leipzig, 1902).

77. The order of true widows was in existence before II Timothy was written. The author was seeking to restrict the conditions of membership to elderly and well-tested women. This seems to support the idea that the letter was written in Paul's name by a later author who was seeking to reduce an all-too-popular alternative.

78. Galatians 3:27-29. The ramifications of this notice have been explored in Wayne Meeks, "The Image of the Androgyne." R. Scroggs, "Paul and the Eschatalogical Woman Revisited," has argued that Paul was quoting from an early Baptismal formula used by his contemporaries, *Journal of the American Academy of Religion,* 42 (1974): 536.

Chapter Three

1. Tacitus, *Annales.* 15. 43.

2. Clement of Rome, *Address to the Greeks.* 6.

3. Eusebius, *Historia Ecclesiastica.* 3. 17-20.

4. The tradition of her sexual rejection of her husband is recounted by Henri Leclercq, *Les Martyrs,* vol. I (Paris, 1906). Paul Styger, *Die romische Katacomben* (Berlin, 1933), pp. 63-80, notes that an early Christian catacomb was dedicated to her.

5. The position of women as members of two families was first studied for antiquity by N. D. Fustel de Coulanges, *The Ancient City* (Garden City, 1873), pp. 42-56. More broadly it provides the basis for Claude Lévi-Strauss' theories on the social structure as a product of the exchange of women between families, see *The Elementary Structures of Kinship* (Boston, 1969).

6. Percy Corbett, *The Roman Law of Marriage* (Oxford, 1930).

7. Sarah B. Pomeroy, "The Relationship of the Married Woman to her Blood Relatives in Rome," *Ancient Society,* 7: 215-27. Reciprocally, he was dispensed with the obligation to endow her with his own property.

8. Gaius, *Institutes* 1. 144.

9. J. P. V. D. Balsdon, *Roman Women* (New York, 1963).

10. Tacitus, *Annales,* 1. 51. Leo F. Raditsa, "Augustus' Legislation Concerning Marriage, Procreation, Love Affairs and Adultery," *Aufstiege und Niedergang der Römische Welt* 2 (1980): 292-95, discusses the fate of Julia as a cross-generational problem reflecting the rebellion of the young against the hypocrisy of an older generation that had solved the political crises of their age by imposing a fictional restoration of the old constitution and the old morality of an age long past.

11. Suetonius, *Augustus,* 34. Michel Humbert, *Le remariage à Rome* (Milan, 1972) argues that the Augustan marriage laws were intended to extend to all the people, not simply the aristocracy which accounts for the variety of the penalties imposed on the obdurately celibate.

12. For further reflections on the anomalies caused by this condition, see Mary Beard, "The Sexual Status of Vestal Virgins," *Journal of Roman Studies* 70 (1980): 12-27.

13. Sarah Pomeroy, "The Relationship of the Married Woman to her Blood Relatives in Rome."

14. I have argued this more fully in "Wives and Widows in Early Christian Thought," *International Journal of Women's Studies,* 2 (1977): 575-92.

15. Sarah B. Pomeroy, *Goddesses, Whores, Wives and Slaves* (New York, 1975), p. 163. Women who sold goods in the market place and who owned small businesses, however, were penalized by being placed beyond the control of the sexual laws as women with whom men could enjoy *stuprum* without suffering penalties, Raditsa, "Augustus' Legislation," p. 314, notes that this sharp separation of the "good" women from the "bad" tended to impose a classification upon the relationships of Roman men with women that effectively forbade the development of genuine love relationships.

16. For a recent discussion of women's education, see Sarah B. Pomeroy, "Women in Roman Egypt," in Helena Foley, *Reflections of Women in Antiquity,* (London, 1981), pp. 303-22; and, by the same author, "Technikai kai Mousikai: The Education of Women in the Fourth Century and in the Hellenistic Period," *American Journal of Ancient History* 2 (1977): 51-68.

17. Juvenal, *Satires* 6. 450-60.

18. Pomeroy, *Goddesses, Whores, Wives and Slaves,* p. 160, points out that Tiberius had to prohibit noble Roman women from registering as prostitutes to escape the adultery laws. Raditsa, "Augustus' Legislation," p. 295, suggests that actions such as these, coupled with the publicity with which Julia and her circle conducted their love affairs, suggests the working out of an ideology of free love intended to make a larger public statement.

19. Justin Martyr, *Apology* 1. 27, in *Works* (New York, 1948).

20. Juvenal, *Satire* 6. 315-20.

21. See the perceptive analysis of these charges by Norman Cohn, *Europe's Inner Demons,* (New York, 1975), pp. 1-15.

22. See particularly Peter Brown, "Sorcery, Demons and the Rise of Christianity," in Mary Douglas, *Witchcraft Confessions and Accusations* (London, 1970), pp. 17-45.

23. Apuleius, *The Golden Ass* (New York, 1919).

24. Pomeroy, *Goddesses, Whores, Wives and Slaves,* p. 217.

25. Justin Martyr made reference to a case in second century Rome where a woman was turned over to the executioners as a Christian when she refused to emulate her husband's licentious life, *Apology* 1. 13.

26. Most notably J. P. V. D. Balsdon, *Roman Women,* who compares the sexual attitudes of Christians very unfavorably with their pagan Roman contemporaries.

27. I am here following the model developed by Mary Douglas, *Purity and Danger,* (New York, 1966), p. 38.

28. Juvenal, *Satires,* 6. 525-30.

29. Propertius 2. 33; 4. 5, 34, *Works,* Loeb Classical Library (Cambridge, Mass, 1952).

30. Robert E. A. Palmer, "Roman shrines of female chastity from the caste struggle to the papacy of Innocent I,' *Rivista storica dell'antichità* 4 (1974): 294-309.

31. These are among the possible alternatives advanced by Douglas, *Purity and Danger,* p. 39.

32. I Corinthians 6:15.

33. The possibility that Priscilla may have written the anonymous *Epistle to the Hebrews* was first suggested by A. Harnack, "Probabilia über die Addresse und der Verfasser des Hebräerbriefe," *Zeitschrift für Neutestamentliche Wissenschaft,* vol. 1 (1900), pp. 16-41. It has been expanded recently by Ruth Hoppin, *Priscilla, Author of the Epistle to the Hebrews* (Philadelphia, 1969).

34. Epistle to the Philippians 7, *The Apostolic Fathers,* Loeb Classical Library (London, 1912).

35. *Pastor,* 1. 1, 1, *Sources Chrétiennes,* vol. 53 (Paris, 1958).

36. Epistle to the Antiochans, 9. Ante Nicene Fathers, vol. 1.

37. Pseudo-Clementine Homilies, 13. 17, Ante Nicene Fathers, vol. 8.

38. Homily 13, 18.

39. II Timothy 3:6. The gnostic gospels preserved in the Nag Hammadi Library echo this same tendency and lay special stress on the prediction that in the Resurrection there will be no marriage or giving in marriage.

40. I Timothy 2:15.

41. Colossians 3:18-25.

42. *Pastor* 7. 2.

43. Ephesians 5:21-33.

44. I Timothy 5:4-8.

45. Colossians 3:20-21; Ephesians 6:4.

46. *Pastor* 2. 1-4.

47. *Epistle to Polycarp* 2. 5.

48. *Pastor* 3. Similitudes 9. 11; Visions 1. 7, 2.

49. *Epistle to Polycarp,* 5.

50. *Epistle to the Smyrnaeans,* Conclusion.

51. Ignatius, *Epistle to the Philadelphians* 4. Philadelphia, we might recall, was the home of the prophetess Ammia who must have been preaching at about this time. This church was also one that Ignatius was concerned to guard from a tendency to Docetism.

52. I Timothy 6:3; Titus 2:8-15; also the *Epistle of Jude.*

53. Revelations 2:20.

54. pseudo-Clement of Rome, *On Virginity,* 1. 10.

55. Ibid., 2. 1.

56. Ibid., 2. 2.

57. Spurious Ignatian Correspondence, 43, Ante Nicene Fathers, vol. 1.

58. Ibid., 3.

59. *To the Philadelphians* 4.

60. I Timothy 2:8.

61. Titus 2:1-5.

62. I Timothy 3:11.

63. *Didache, Ante Nicene Fathers* vol. 7.

64. Spurious Ignatian Correspondence, Ante Nicene Fathers vols. 1, 126; see also Jean Higgins, "Fidelity to History," in Leonard Swidler and Arlene Swidler, *Women Priests* (New York, 1977).

65. *Address to the Greeks,* 4.

66. Ibid., 40.

67. *Epistle to the Philippians,* 5.

68. *Canones Apostolorum* 24-28, in *Monumenta de viduis, diaconissis, virginibusque tractantia* (Bonn, 1938).

69. *Didascalia et Constitutiones Apostolorum,* 2. 15 (Paderborn, 1905).

70. I Timothy 3:11.

71. I Timothy 2:8-15.

72. Titus 2:1-5.
73. *Pastor* 1, 1, 4.
74. *Canones Apostolorum* 1. 51.

Chapter Four

1. This is what happened in the celebrated case reported to the Emperor Trajan by Pliny the Younger, *Epistola* 96, *Letters and Panegyrics,* Loeb Classical Library (Cambridge, Mass, 1969).

2. See Marie Meunier, *Femmes Pythagoriciennes,* (Paris, 1932).

3. Origen, *Contra Celsum* 3. 55, elaborated by E. R. Dodd, *Pagan and Christian in an Age of Anxiety,* (Cambridge, 1965), p. 116.

4. Eusebius, *Historia Ecclesiastica* 6. 3, *Sources Chrétiennes* vol. 41 (Paris, 1954).

5. Tacitus, *Annales* 13. 32, 2 records the indulgence of a husband whose wife was accused of "foreign superstition." He exercised his familial authority to try her privately and acquit her.

6. Hippolytus, *Refutation of all Heresies* 6. 15 Ante Nicene Fathers vol. 5.

7. The connection between the establishment of the episcopal hierarchy and the formulation of orthodox dictrine has been laid out by Elaine Pagels in her provocative book *The Gnostic Gospels* (New York, 1979).

8. Irenaeus, *Adversus Haereses* 1, 13, 7, *Sources Chrétiennes* vol. 34 (Paris, 1952).

9. *Acts of Paul and Thecla,* Ante Nicene Fathers vol. 8, p. 490.

10. A detailed summary of gnostic teaching would not serve the purposes of this book. Some of their treatises have been preserved in J. M. Robinson, *The Nag Hammadi Library* (New York, 1977) and a systematic coverage of their ideas is provided by Hans Jonas, *The Gnostic Religion* (Boston, 1959).

11. For example, the *Gospel of Truth* 24, *Nag Hammadi Library,* p. 41 says that the divine triad is "the father, the mother and Jesus of infinite gentleness." But, in contrast, the *First Stele of Seth,* p. 363, praises the perfection of the three-fold male.

12. *Exegesis of the Soul, Nag Hammadi Library,* p. 181.

13. Hippolytus, *Refutation of all Heresies,* 14.

14. Epiphanius, *Adversus Haereses* 1. 45, 2, *Opera* (Leipzig, 1859).

15. Irenaeus, *Adversus Haereses* 2. 27.

16. *Dialogue of the Savior, Nag Hammadi Library,* p. 238.

17. *Gospel of Philip, Nag Hammadi Library,* p. 137.

18. *Exegesis of the Soul, Nag Hammadi Library,* p. 184.

19. Stevan Davies, *The Revolt of the Widows* (Carbondale, IL, 1980) connects these attitudes to social deviance.

20. Hippolytus, *Refutation of all Heresies* 7. 26. Also Tertullian, *De Praescriptiones Haereses* 6 and 30, *Opera* (Turnholt, 1954).

21. They were still operating in the fourth century when Epiphanius encountered them: *Panarion* 78. 23; 79, 2-4, *Opera* (Leipzig, 1959-62).

22. Pagels, *The Gnostic Gospels* pp. 49 ff. pursued this problem interpreting the gnostic gospels as the champions of the prophetic faction. See particularly, her introduction to the "Letter of Peter to Philip," *Nag Hammadi Library,* p. 427.

23. *De Praescriptiones Haereses* 41, 5.

24. *De Baptismo* 17, *Opera* (Turnholt, 1954).

25. Cited by Cyprian, *Epistola* 74, *Opera* (Turnholt, 1976).

26. Henri Graillot, *Le Culte de Cybèle à Rome et dans l'Empire Romain* (Paris, 1912), p. 404.

27. Hippolytus, *Philosophumena* 8. 19, *Sources Chrétiennes* vol. 6 (Paris, 1928).

28. Eusebius, *Historia Ecclesiastica* 5. 16. See also, Elizabeth Fiorenza, "Word, Spirit and Power," pp. 29-70.

29. *Ad Uxorem* 1. 6, *Opera* (Turnholt, 1954).

30. *De monogamia*, (Turnholt, 1954).
31. *Historia Ecclesiastica* 5. 18.
32. Hippolytus, *Refutation of all Heresies*, 8, 12.
33. "Clement of Rome," *Letter on Virginity* 5.
34. Ibid.
35. *The Martyrdom of the Holy Martyrs Justin, Chariton, Charites, Paeon and Liberanius, who suffered at Rome*, 3, Ante Nicene Fathers, vol. 1, p. 306.
36. This process has been clearly discerned in the fourth century by Peter Brown, "Aspects of the Christianization of Roman Society," in *Religion and Society in the Age of Augustine* (London, 1972), pp. 161-82.
37. *Address to the Greeks* 40.
38. Justin Martyr, *Apologia* 1. 13, *Works* (New York, 1948).
39. *Epistola* 96.
40. Justin Martyr, *Apologia* 1, 65.
41. Apostolic Constitutions 3. 15, 2, in *Didascalia et Constitutiones Apostolorum* (Paderborn, 1905).
42. Pliny, *Epistola* 96.
43. Homily 2. 15 Ante Nicene Fathers vol. 8, had already expounded a "doctrine of pairs" in the natural order characterized by the precedence of the weaker and negative partner destined to be overcome by the stronger "masculine" element.
44. Homily 3. 23.
45. The trend itself is amply described by Bernard Prusak, "Use the Other Door; Stand at the End of the Line," in Leonard and Arlene Swidler, *Woman Priests*, pp. 81-85.
46. Clement of Alexandria, *Stromata* 4. 1, *Sources Chrétiennes* vols. 30, 38 (Paris, 1951-54).
47. Tatian, *Address to the Greeks*, 33, Ante Nicene Fathers vol. 10.
48. *De Anima* 9 *Opera* (Turnholt, 1954). It is possible that this practice of cross-examination occurred in a Montanist congregation. The sister would probably have been less respectfully treated in a more orthodox community at this time. But it is a debatable point.
49. *Dialogue* 88, 1.
50. *Epistola* 74 (75), Ante Nicene Fathers vol. 5.
51. Carolyn Oisek, "The Church Fathers and the Ministry of Women," in L. and A. Swidler, *Women Priests*, pp. 75-81.
52. See editions by Montague R. James, *The Apocryphal New Testament* (Oxford, 1972) and Edgar Hennecke and Wilhelm Schneemelcher, *New Testament Apocrypha*, 2 vols. (Philadelphia, 1963-65).
53. S. P. Brock, "Early Syrian Asceticism," *Numen* 20 (1972): 1-19.
54. This argument has won general acceptance though there is still disagreement on the dating of these works as discussed by E. Neubert, *Marie dans l'église antenicéene* (Paris, 1980), and most recently summarized by Stevan Davies in the first chapter of *The Revolt of the Widows* (Carbondale, IL: 1980).
55. This theory has been most powerfully advanced by S. Davies, *Revolt*, chapter 6, to whom I owe many of the ideas taken up in this section. For a more general statement on works written by women at this time see Sarah Pomeroy, "Technikai kai Mousikai."
56. *Acts of Bartholomew*, in M. R. James, *Apocryphal New Testament* (Oxford, 1972), p. 170.
57. *Acts of Pilate* 12, in James, *Apocryphal New Testament*.
58. For a full discussion of doctrines concerning Mary in this period see E. Neubert, *Marie dans l'église antenicéene* (Paris, 1908).
59. *Protoevangelion*, 2. 2 in James, Apocryphal New Testament.
60. Ibid., 8, 3-7.
61. Ibid., 8.
62. Ibid., 20.
63. *Acts of Bartholomew* 2, in James, *Apocryphal New Testament*, p. 170.
64. Ibid., pp. 183 ff.

65. Ibid., pp. 194-227.

66. Ibid., p. 194.

67. Ibid., pp. 194-227.

68. Ibid., p. 266.

69. Ibid., p. 269.

70. Ibid., *Acts of Paul* 5-12.

71. *Acts of Peter* 1, in James *Apocryphal New Testament,* pp. 300-36.

72. *Acts of John* 51-63, in James, *Apocryphal New Testament,* p. 253.

73. "Preface," *The Plays of Hroswitha,* (New York, 1966), p. xxvi.

74. James, *Apocryphal New Testament,* pp. 82 ff.

75. Trophime, *Acts of Andrew* 23 and Maximilla, from a fragment of "Andrew" cited by James from Evodius, *Apocryphal New Testament.*

76. The most dramatic examplar of this theme was Thecla. James, *Apocryphal New Testament,* p.272, argues that she may indeed have been a genuine local martyr whose story later became attached to Paul's. Certainly, Queen Tryphaena, who intervenes as her protector when she is threatened with martyrdom, was a real person, the widow of the King of Thrace, mother of the King of Pontus and grandniece of the Emperor Claudius.

77. *Acts of Thomas* 1. 12.

78. Ibid., 6.61; see also *Acts of Andrew* 25: in a primitive version of the type of miracle called the "abbess delivered" by Giles Constable, "Aelred of Rievaulx and the Nun of Watton," in Derek Baker, *Medieval Women* (Oxford, 1978), pp. 205-226, a woman prayed to Diana for help in delivering the illegitimate child whose father was a murderer. In exchange for her repentance, Andrew arranged that the child be born dead.

79. *Apology to the Senate* 2. 2.

Chapter Five

1. Eusebius, *Historia Ecclesiastica.* 5. 1, 7, *Sources Chrétiennes* vol. 41 (Paris, 1954).

2. *The Passion of Perpetua and Felicity,* 10, ed. W. H. Shewring (London, 1931). For a discussion of Perpetua's possible gnostic tendencies and sexual ambivalence, see E. R. Dodd, *Pagan and Christian in an Age of Anxiety* (Cambridge, 1965), p. 112.

3. For a discussion of this tradition, see R. B. Tollinton, *Clement of Alexandria, A Study in Christian Liberalism* (London, 1914), p. 285.

4. Eusebius, *Historia Ecclesiastica* 21. 3-4, *Sources Chrétiennes* vol. 41 (Paris: 1954).

5. Ibid., 5. 1, 11.

6. Ibid., 5. 25-26.

7. Ibid., 6. 3, 1-3.

8. Clement of Alexandria, *Paedagogus* 3. 4 *Sources Chrétiennes* vols. 70, 108, 158 (Paris, 1960-70).

9. Ibid., 4.

10. This rejection of the double standard was later to become a commonplace in patristic literature, see J. McNamara, "Sexual Equality and the Cult of Virginity in Early Christian Thought," *Feminist Studies* 3 (1976): 3-4, 145-58.

11. *Paedagogus* 1. 4.

12. *Stromata* 4. 8 *Sources Chretiénnes,* vols. 30, 38 (Paris, 1951-54).

13. *Paedagogus* 3. 12. In this context, Clement's reference to women who could dispense with the veil if they were at home reminds us that even in Alexandria with its several churches some women must still have been supporting churches in their homes, or perhaps forming a congregation from the members of their *familia.*

14. *Didascalia et Constitutiones Apostolorum,* 6. 27, ed. F. X. Funk, (Paderborn, 1905).

15. Justin Martyr, *Apologia* 1. 29 *Works, Fathers of the Church* vol. 6 (New York, 1948).

16. *Stromata* 3. 1.

17. Ibid., 3. 10.

18. *Paedagogus* 2, 10.

19. *Stromata* 2. 23.

20. Tertullian, *Ad Uxorem* 2, *Opera,* (Turnholt, 1954).

21. *Stromata* 4. 8. Well-trained as Clement was in traditional philosophy, he may well have been borrowing this idea from Plato, *Republic* 5 without noting the debt. In general, however, the Christian theologians appear to have believed that agreement between their ideas and those of pagan philosophers only provided confirmation of the truth of their arguments and were, therefore, not shy about borrowing where they could.

22. *Stromata* 3. 6.

23. Ibid., 3. 33.

24. Ibid., 3. 2.

25. Ibid., 3. 4.

26. Ibid., 4. 8.

27. Ibid., 4. 19.

28. *Paedagogus* 3. 11.

29. Ibid.

30. Clement, *Stromata* 4. 18 and Tertullian, *Ad Uxorem* 2. 5.

31. Cyprian, *Epistola* 24, *Opera* (Turnholt, 1972-76).

32. For a systematic account of these and other martyrs of the period, see Henri Leclercq, *Les Martyres,* vol. 1, (Paris: 1906).

33. *Ad Uxorem* 2. 8.

34. Tertullian, *De Carne Christu, Opera* (Turnholt, 1954), argued that Mary's virginity ended after Christ's birth. These and similar opinions of the period are cited by H. Koch, *Adhuc Virgo: Mariens Jungfrauschaft und Ehe in der alt kirchlichen Überlieferung bis zum Ende des 4. Jahrhunderts* (Tübingen, 1929), who advances the opinion that the point was not established in (male) theology until the fourth century.

35. Cyprian, *De habitu virginum* 4, *Opera* (Turnholt, 1972-76).

36. Tertullian, *De cultu feminarum* 1. 1 *Opera* (Turnholt, 1954).

37. Cyprian, *Epistola* 40. 1.

38. *Didascalia et Constitutiones Apostolorum* 3. 17.

39. Ibid., 2. 2.

40. *Stromata* 3. 6.

41. *Stromata* 3. 9.

42. Justin Martyr, *Apologia* 1. 15.

43. Origen, *Commentaire sur l'evangèle selon Matthieu* 22, *Sources Chrétiennes* vol. 162 (Paris, 1970).

44. *Stromata* 3. 12 and 18.

45. Eusebius, *Historia Ecclesiastica* 6. 3, 9-13.

46. Origen, *Homily on Leviticus* 6. 6.

47. Eusebius, *Historia Ecclesiastica* 24. 6-7.

48. Hippolytus, *Adversus Haereses,* 9, 12. 22. For further discussion see E. Pagels, *The Gnostic Gospels* (New York, 1979), p. 89 and for bibliography, J. P. Caudet, *Mariage et célibat dans le service pastoral de l'église.* (Paris, 1967).

49. *Didascalia et Constitutiones Apostolorum* 2. 17.

50. In any case, he denied the Gospel's claim to consideration as a canonical text, *Stromata* 3. 13.

51. *Ad Uxorem* 2. 8.

52. *The Passion of Perpetua and Felicity,* ed. and trans., W. H. Shewring (London, 1931).

Chapter Six

1. Eusebius, *Historia Ecclesiastica* 5. 18, 4, *Sources Chrétiennes* vol. 41 (Paris, 1954).

2. The development of this practice cannot be traced in available sources. Like much liturgical development, we discern it only when it is complete. However, the virgins are in

place by the third century as noted in the Apostolic Constitutions, *Didascalia et Constitutiones Apostolorum* 2. 7 (Paderborn, 1905) and by Cyprian and his contemporaries in their various tracts regulating the behavior of the group.

3. Henry Leclercq, *Les Martyres*, vol. 1, (Paris, 1906) gives details and extracts from these legends, the most famous of which concerns the disputed Saint Agnes. Another group of similar stories were preserved by Palladius, *Lausiac History, Ancient Christian Writers*, vol. 34, pp. 145-148.

4. Gregory Thaumaturge, Canonical Epistle 1, Ante Nicene Fathers vol. 6.

5. *De Oratione* 21, *Opera* (Turnholt, 1954).

6. Ibid., 22.

7. Ibid.

8. *De velandi virginum* 9 *Opera* (Turnholt, 1954).

9. *De cultu feminarum* 1, 1 *Opera* (Turnholt, 1954).

10. Ibid., 2. 5.

11. Ibid., 1. 2.

12. Ibid., 2. 1; 2. 8-9. The ascetic violence of Book 1 has generally persuaded scholars that it was produced in Tertullian's Montanist phase. The latest interpreter, Timothy D. Barnes, *Tertullian* (Oxford, 1971), p. 55, suggests that Book 2 is orthodox and was written first.

13. *Didascalia et Constituiones Apostolorum* 2. 2.

14. *De velandi virginum* 7.

15. *De Baptismo*, 17 *Opera* (Turnholt, 1954).

16. *De velandi virginum*, 9.

17. For a survey of this phenomenon, see Vern L. Bullough, "Transvestitism in the Middle Ages," in V. Bullough and J. Brundage, *Sexual Practices in the Medieval Church* (Buffalo, 1982), p. 43-54.

18. *De Ieiunio*, 17 *Opera* (Turnholt, 1954).

19. *Exhortatio castitatis*, 12, *Opera* (Turnholt, 1954).

20. Eusebius, *Historia Ecclesiastica* 7. 30, 12-16.

21. Cyprian, *Epistolae* 4. 1, 1; 3. 3 (Turnholt, 1972-76).

22. Ibid., *Epistola* 4. 3.

23. *Didascalia et Constitutiones Apostolorum* 5. 14.

24. *De cultu feminarum* 2. 2.

25. *De velandi virginum* 14.

26. This is the same justification that modern enforcers of the gender system employ in excusing rape as a crime provoked by its victim. For a full historical and sociological study see Susan Brownmiller, *Against Our Will: Men, Women and Rape* (New York, 1975). The association of provocative clothing with rape was, in fact, enshrined in Roman Law: *Digest*, 47, 10, 15, 15-20.

27. Cyprian, *De habitu virginum*, 5. 15 *Opera* (Turnholt, 1972-76).

28. Ibid., 5, 18.

29. Ibid., 5, 19.

30. This and other efforts to define and control Christian sexuality at Elvira have been carefully scrutinized by Samuel Laeuchli from the point of view of male anxiety, *Power and Sexuality: The Emergence of Canon Law at the Synod of Elvira* (Philadelphia, 1972).

31. *Didascalia et Constitutiones Apostolorum* 2. 1, 2.

32. Eugène de Faye, *Origène: Sa vie, son oeuvre, sa pensèe* (Paris, 1923), p. 33.

33. To be sure, that is a common theme of the great fourth century proponents of virginity. But the whole argument of this book is that these patristic writers were late-comers to the movement.

34. *De velandi virginum* 9.

35. Cyprian, *De habitu virginum* 4.

36. *Didascalia et Constitutiones Apostolorum* 3. 2, 15.

37. Ibid., 3. 9.

38. Ibid., 3. 6.

39. Ibid., 3. 19-25.

40. *De velandi virginum* 17.

41. *De oratione* 25.

42. *Adversus Haereses, Opera* (Leipzig: 1859-62).

43. "Introduction," James Robinson, ed., *The Nag Hammadi Library* (New York, 1977).

44. Nîmes, 2, in C. H. Hefele, *A History of the Councils* (Edinburgh, 1896) vol. 1, p. 93.

45. J. D. Mansi, *Sacrorum Conciliorum Nova et Amplissima Collectio* (Venice, 1780), vol. 3, pp. 693.

46. 19, Ibid., vol. 2, p. 676.

47. *Adversus Haereses* 3. 2, 7. The so-called Council of Carthage, in 398 was often cited in later documents. But Hefele, *History of the Councils,* vol. 2, p. 68, failed to find any genuine record of its proceedings.

48. Methodius, "Introduction," *Symposium,* (Westminster, MD, 1958).

49. Ibid., 1. 5.

50. *Exhortatio castitatis* 1.

51. *Didascalia et Constitutiones Apostolorum* 2, 7.

52. Gregory Thaumaturge, *Homily* 2; Geoffrey Ashe, *The Virgin* (London, 1976), p. 177, relates these ideas of Gregory to those of his successors in Cappadoccia, Basil, Gregory of Nyssa and Gregory Nazianzus, who were leaders in the fourth century development of the cult of the virgin in the area.

53. *De habitu virginum* 3.

54. *Ad uxorem* 1. 4.

55. *Symposium,* Discourse 2.

56. Ibid., Discourse 1. 5.

Conclusion

1. Methodius, *Symposium,* Discourse 5, "Thalousa," 4, *Ancient Christian Writers,* vol. 27 (Westminster, MD, 1958).

2. Ibid., Discourse 7, "Procilla" 9.

3. Ibid., 2. 1; 2. 3, 4, 23.

Bibliography

Where available, I have appended references to English translations to the bibliographical citations.

Achelis, H. *Virgines subintroductae.* Leipzig, 1902.

Apuleius Madaurensis. *The Golden Ass.* Includes translation by W. Adlington. New York, 1919.

Ashe, Geoffrey. *The Virgin.* London, 1976.

Babylonian Talmud, trans. by I. Epstein. London, 1935.

Balsdon, J. P. V. D. *Roman Women.* New York, 1963.

Barnes, Timothy D. *Tertullian.* Oxford, 1971.

Baron, Salo. *Religious and Social History of the Jews.* Vol. 2, New York, 1952.

Bauer, J. B. "Uxores circumducere." *Biblische Zeitschrift,* n.s. 3 (1959): 94-102.

Beard, Mary. "The Sexual Status of Vestal Virgins." *Journal of Roman Studies,* 70 (1980): 12-27.

Beauvoir, Simone de. *The Second Sex.* New York, 1974.

Bettencourt, S. T. "Doctrina Ascetica Origenis." *Studia Anselmiana* 16 (1945): 120-129.

Boehmer, H. "Die Entstehung des Zölibates." *Geschichtliche Studien Albert Hauck zum 70. Geburtstage dargebrucht.* Leipzig, 1916, pp. 6-24.

Bouché-Leclercq, J. "Les lois demographiques d'Auguste." *Revue Historique* 57 (1895): 241-92.

Boucher, Madeleine. "Some unexplored parallels to I Cor. 11-12 and Gal. 3:28: The New Testament on the Role of Women." *Catholic Biblical Quarterly* 31 (1969): 50-58.

Brock, S. P. "Early Syrian Asceticism." *Numen* 20 (1972): 1-19.

Brodéhoux, J. P. *Mariage et famille chez Clement d'Alexandrie.* Paris, 1970.

Brown, Peter. "Aspects of the Christianization of the Roman Aristocracy." In *Religion and Society in the Age of Saint Augustine.* London, 1972, pp. 161-182.

Brown, R. E., Donfield, K. P., Fitzmyer, J. A., Reumann, J. eds. *Mary in the New Testament.* Philadelphia, New York, 1978.

Bugge, John. *Virginitas: An Essay in the History of a Medieval Ideal.* The Hague, 1975.

Bullough, Vern L. and Brundage, James A. *Sexual Practices and the Medieval Church.* Buffalo, New York, 1982.

Burrows, Millar. *Dead Sea Scrolls.* New York, 1955.

Cameron, Averil. "Neither Male nor Female," *Greece and Rome.* 2nd ser. 27, (1980): 60-68.

Campbell, B. "The Marriage of Soldiers Under the Empire." *Journal of Roman Studies* 68 (1978): 153-66.

Campbell, J. A. "Virgins Consecrated to God in Rome During the First Centuries." *American Catholic Quarterly Review* 25 (1900): 766-799.

Carmichael, Calum M. *Women, Law and the Genesis Tradition.* New York, 1979.

Cassuto, Ugo. *A Contemporary on the Book of Genesis.* Translated by I. Abraham. Jerusalem, n.d.

Caudet, Jean Paul. *Mariage et célibat dans le service pastoral de l'église.* Paris, 1967.

Chanson, Paul. *Le mariage chrétien selon Saint Paul.* Paris, 1953.

Christ, Carol P. and Plaskow, Judith. *Womanspirit Rising.* San Francisco, 1979.

Clement of Alexandria, *Paedagogus, Sources Chrétiennes* vols. 70, 108, 158. Paris, 1960-70. *Christ the Educator.* Translated by S. P. Wood. *Fathers of the Church.* New York, 1954.

Clement of Alexandria. *Stromata, Sources Chrétiennes.* vols. 30, 38. Paris, 1951-54.

Clement of Rome. *Address to the Greeks.* Translated by F. X. Cima. *Fathers of the Church.* New York, 1947.

Clement of Rome. *Two Epistles Concerning Virginity.* Ante Nicene Fathers, vol. 14. Grand Rapids, 1975.

Cohen, Shaye J. D. "Women in the Synagogues of Antiquity," *Conservative Judaism,* 34, 2 (1980): 23-29.

Cohn, Norman. *Europe's Inner Demons.* New York, 1975.

Constable, Giles, "Aelred of Rievaulx and the Nun of Watton: An Episode in the Early History of the Gilbertine order." In Baker, Derek, ed. *Medieval Women.* Oxford, 1978.

Corbett, Percy E. *The Roman Law of Marriage.* Oxford, 1930.

Crownfield, F. R. *A Historical Approach to the New Testament.* New York, 1960.

Cyprian of Carthage. *Sancti Cypriani episcopi opera.* Corpus Christianorum. Series Latina. 3 vols. Turnholt, 1972-76. *Letters.* Translated by R. Bernard. Washington, 1964. *De habitu virginum.* Translated by A. E. Keenan. Washington, 1932.

Dagron, Gilbert. *Vie et miracles de sainte Thècla. Subsidia Hagiographica* vol. 62, Bruxelles, 1978.

Dauvilliers, J. *Les temps apostolique. Histoire du droit et des institutions de l'église en occident,* vol. 2, Paris, 1970.

Davies, Stevan. *The Revolt of the Widows: the Social World of the Apocryphal Acts.* Carbondale, 1980.

Didache, Ante Nicene Fathers vol. 7, pp. 377-82.

Didascalia et Constitutiones Apostolorum. Edited by F. X. Funk. Paderborn, 1905.

Dodds, E. R. *Pagan and Christian in an Age of Anxiety.* Cambridge, 1965.

Douglas, Mary. *Purity and Danger.* New York and Washington, 1966.

Douglas, Mary, ed. *Witchcraft Confessions and Accusations.* London and New York, 1970.

Epiphanius. *Adversus Haereses, Opera.* Edited by G. Dinforfius. Leipzig, 1859-62.

Eusebius. *Historia Ecclesiastica. Sources Chretiénnes* vol. 41. Paris, 1954. Translated by R. J. Deferrari, The Fathers of the Church, vols. 28-29. New York, 1955.

Eusebius. *Evangelica Praeparatione. Sources Chretiénnes* vol. 206. Paris, 1974.

Farmer, William R. *The Synoptic Problem: A Critical Analysis.* Macon, Georgia, 1981.

Faye, Eugène de. *Origène: Sa vie, son oeuvre, sa pensée.* Paris, 1923.

Field, J. A., Jr. "The Purpose of the Lex Julia et Papia Poppaea." *Classical Journal,* 40 (1944-45): 398-416.

Foley, Helena. *Reflections of Women in Antiquity.* London, 1981.

Fritsch, Charles T. *The Qumran Community: Its History and Scrolls.* New York, 1956.

Fustel de Coulanges, N. D. *The Ancient City.* Garden City, 1873.

Gager, J. G. *Kingdom and Community: The Social World of Early Christianity.* Englewood Cliffs, NJ, 1975.

de Gaiffier, B. "Intactam sponsam relinquens." *Analecta Bollandiana* 75 (1947): 157-95; 83 (1965): 468-77.

Gaius. *Institutiones.* Edited by E. Seckel and B. Keubler. Leipzig, 1935; *Institutes.* Oxford, 1946.

Gaudemet, J. "Observations sur la manus." *Revue Internationale des droit de l'Antiquité* 2 (1953).

Goppelt, Leonhard. *Apostolic and Post-Apostolic Times.* Translated by R. A. Guelich, London, 1970.

Graillot, Henri. *Le culte de Cybèle, mère des dieux, à Rome et dans l'Empire romain.* Paris, 1912.

Grant, Robert M. *Gnosticism and Early Christianity.* New York, 1959.

Gregory Thaumaturge. *Works.* Ante Nicene Fathers. Vol. 6. Grand Rapids, 1975.

Gryson, Roger. *Les origines du célibat ecclésiastique du première au septième siècles.* Gembloux, 1970.

Gryson, Roger. "Le ministère des femmes dans l'église ancienne." Recherches et synthèses. Sec. d'histoire 4. Gembloux, 1972.

Guignebert, Charles. *The Jewish World in the Time of Jesus.* New York, 1959.

Harnack, A. "Probabilia über die Addresse und den Verfasser des Hebräerbriefes." *Zeitschrift fur Neutestamentliche Wissenschaft* 1, pp. 16-41.

Hefele, C. H. *A History of the Councils.* Translated by H. N. Oxenham. Edinburgh, 1896.

Hempel, J. "Beobachtungen an der 'syrischen' Jesujarolle vom Toten Meer." *Zeitschrift der deutsch Morgenländischen Gesellschaft.* (1951): 138-73.

Hennecke, Edgar and Schneemelcher, Wilhelm. *New Testament Apocrypha.* Philadelphia, 1963-65.

Hermas. *Pastor. Sources chrétiennes* vol. 53. Paris, 1958; Translated in Ante Nicene Fathers, vol. 2. Grand Rapids, 1975.

Hinchcliff, Peter B. *Cyprian of Carthage and the Unity of the Christian Church.* London, 1974.

Hippolytus. *Philosophumena, or Réfutation de toutes les hérésies, Sources Chrétiennes,* vol. 6. Paris, 1928; Translated in Ante Nicene Fathers, vol. 6. Grand Rapids, 1975.

Hoppin, Ruth. *Priscilla, Author of the Epistle to the Hebrews.* Philadelphia, 1969.

Humbert, Michel. *Le remariage à Rome.* Milan, 1972.

Ignatius. *Epistles.* Ante Nicene Fathers, vol. 1, pp. 45-127.

Irenaeus of Lyon. *Contre les hérésies. Sources Chrétiennes,* vol. 34. Paris, 1952; Translated in Ante Nicene Fathers, vol. 1. Grand Rapids, 1975.

James, Montague R. *The Apocryphal New Testament.* Oxford, 1972.

Jonas, Hans. *The Gnostic Religion.* Boston, 1959.

Josephus, Flavius. *Jewish War and Jewish Antiquities.* Loeb Classical Library, vols. 2-9, London, 1926.

Justin Martyr. *Works.* Translated by T. B. Falls. The Fathers of the Church, vol. 6. New York, 1948.

Juvenal. *Satires.* Edited and translated by G. G. Ramsay. Loeb Classical Library. London, 1924.

Koch, Hugo. *Adhuc Virgo: Mariens Jungfrauschaft und Ehe in der alt kirchlichen Überlieferung bis zum Ende des 4. Jahrhunderts.* Tubingen, 1929.

Koch, Hugo. *Virgines Christi: De Gelübde der gottgewichten Jungfrauen in den ersten drei Jahrhunderten. Texte und untersuchungen zur Geschichte der altchristlichen Literatur* 31 (1907): 62-112.

Koch, Hugo. *Virgo Eva—Virgo Maria. Neue Untersuchungen über die Lehre von der Jungfrauschaft und der Ehe Mariens in der ältesten Kirche. Arbeiten zur Kirchengeschichte,* vol. 25. Berlin, 1937.

Kraemer, Ross. "The Conversion of Women to Ascetic Forms of Christianity." *Signs* 6 (1981): 298-307.

Labriolle, Pierre de. "La mariage spirituel dans l'antiquité chrétienne." *Revue Historique* 137 (1921): 204-225.

Labriolle, Pierre de. *La crise montanism.* Fribourg, 1913.

Laeuchli, Samuel. *Power and Sexuality: The Emergence of Canon Law at the Synod of Elvira.* Philadelphia, 1972.

Leclercq, H. *Les martyres.* Vols. 1 and 2. Paris, 1906 and 1909.

Legrand, Lucien. *The Biblical Doctrine of Virginity.* New York, 1963.

Lehner, F. A. *Die Marienverehrung in der ersten Jahrhunderten.* Stuttgard, 1886.

Leipoldt, J. *Die Frau in der Antiken Welt und im Urchristentum.* Leipzig, 1954.

Leon, Harry J. *Jews of Ancient Rome.* Philadelphia, 1960.

Lévi-Strauss, Claude. *The Elementary Structures of Kinship.* Boston, 1969.

Lewis, Ioan M. *Ecstatic Religion.* Penguin Books, 1971.

Lightman, Marjorie, and Zeisel, William. "Univira," *Church History.* 46 (1977): 19-32.

Lynch, John E. "Marriage and Celibacy of the Clergy: The Discipline of the Western

Church: A Historico-Canonical Synopsis." *The Jurist.* 32 (1972) part 1: 14-38; part 2: 189-312.

Mansi, Johannes D. *Sacrorum Conciliorum nova et Amplissima Collectio.* Venice, 1780.

McHugh, John. *The Mother of Jesus in the New Testament.* Garden City, 1975.

McNamara, Jo Ann. "Sexual Equality and the Cult of Virginity in Early Christian Thought." *Feminist Studies* 3 (1976): 145-58.

McNamara, Jo Ann. "Wives and Widows in Early Christian Thought." *International Journal of Women's Studies* 2 (1977): 575-592.

Meeks, Wayne A. "The Image of the Androgyne: Some Uses of a Symbol in Earliest Christianity." *History of Religions* 13 (1974): 165-208.

Messing, S. "Group Therapy and Social Status in the Zar Cult of Ethiopia." In John Middleton, ed., *Magic, Witchcraft, and Curing.* Austin, 1967, pp. 285-294.

Methodius. *The Symposium: A Treatise on Chastity.* Translated by H. Musurilla. Ancient Christian Writers, vol. 27. Westminster, MD, 1958.

Metz, René. "Les conditions juridiques de la consecration des vièrges." *Revue de droit canonique* 1 (1951).

Meunier, Marie. *Femmes Pythagoriciennes, Fragments et Lettres de Théano, Périctioné, Mélissa et Myia.* Paris, 1932.

Mishnah. Translated by Herbert Danby. London, 1938.

Monumenta de viduis, diaconissis, virginibusque tractantia. Edited by J. Mayer. *Florilegium Patristicum,* vol. 42. Bonn, 1938.

Neubert, E. *Marie dans l'église antenicéenne.* Paris, 1908.

Neusner, Jacob. *A History of the Mishnaic Law of Women.* Studies in Judiasm in Late Antiquity, vol. 33. Leiden, 1980.

Nugent, M. Rosamond. *Portrait of the Consecrated Woman in Greek Christian Literature of the First Four Centuries.* Washington, 1941.

Origen. *Commentaire sur l'evangile selon Matthieu 22, Sources Chrétiennes,* vol. 162. Paris, 1970. Translated with *Fragment on 1 Cor. 74* and *Homily on Leviticus,* Ante Nicene Fathers, vol. 4. Grand Rapids, 1976.

Origen. *Contra Celsum,* Ante Nicene Fathers, vol. 4. Grand Rapids, 1976.

Pagels, Elaine. *The Gnostic Gospels.* New York, 1979.

Palladius. *The Lausiac History.* Edited and translated by Robert T. Meyer. *Ancient Christian Writers,* vol. 34. Westminster, MD, n.d.

Palmer, Robert E. A. "Roman Shrines of Female Chastity from the Caste Struggle to the Papacy of Innocent I." *Rivista Storica dell'Antichità,* 4 (1974): 294-309.

Passion of Perpetua and Felicity, together with the Sermons of Saint Augustine on these Saints. Edited and translated by W. H. Shewring. London, 1931.

Philo of Alexandria. *Works.* Edited and translated by F. H. Colson and G. H. Whitaker. Loeb Classical Library. Cambridge, MA, 1962.

Phipps, William E. *Was Jesus Married?* New York, 1970.

Pliny the Elder. *Historia Naturalis.* Loeb Classical Library. Cambridge, MA, 1938-63.

Pliny the Younger. *Letters and Panegyrics.* Edited and translated by Betty Radice. Loeb Classical Library. Cambridge, MA, 1969.

Polycarp of Smyrna and Ignatius of Antioch. *Lettres. Sources Chrétiennes,* vol. 10. Paris, 1958. Polycarp, *The Apostolic Fathers.* Edited and translated by K. Lake. Loeb Classical Library. London, 1912.

Pomeroy, Sarah B. *Goddesses, Whores, Wives and Slaves.* New York, 1975.

Pomeroy, Sarah B. "Technikai kai Mousikai: The Education of Women in the Fourth Century and in the Hellenistic Period." *American Journal of Ancient History* 2 (1977): 51-68.

Pomeroy, Sarah B. "The Relationship of the Married Woman to her Blood Relatives in Rome." *Ancient Society* 7, 215-27.

Propertius, Sextus Aurelius. *Works.* Edited and translated by H. E. Butler. Loeb Classical Library. Cambridge, MA, 1952.

Pseudo-Clementine Homilies. Ante Nicene Fathers, vol. 8. Grand Rapids, 1951.

Quéré-Jaulmes, F. *Le mariage dans l'église ancienne.* Paris, 1969.

Raditsa, Leo F. "Augustus' Legislation Concerning Marriage, Procreation, Love Affairs and Adultery." *Aufstiege und Niedergang der Römische Welt* 2, (1980): 278-339.

Robinson, James M., ed. *The Nag Hammadi Library.* New York, 1977.

Robinson, John A. T. *Re-dating the New Testament.* London, 1976.

Roby, Henry J. *Roman Private Law.* Cambridge, 1902.

Rosambert, A. *La veuve en droit canonique.* Paris, 1923.

Ruether, Rosemary R., ed. *Religion and Sexism.* New York, 1974.

Ruether, Rosemary R. and McLaughlin, Eleanor C. *Women of Spirit: Female Leadership in the Jewish and Christian Traditions.* New York, 1979.

Sandmel, Samuel. *The First Christian Centuries in Judaism and Christianity.* New York, 1969.

Schillebeeckx, E. *Celibacy.* New York, 1968.

Schulz, Fritz. *Classical Roman Law.* Oxford, 1951.

Schurer, Emil. *The History of the Jewish People in the Age of Jesus Christ.* Rev. ed., New York, 1978.

Scroggs, R. "Paul and the Eschatalogical Woman Revisited." *Journal of the American Academy of Religion* 42 (1974): 536.

Showalter, Elaine. *A Literature of Their Own.* Princeton, 1977.

Smallwood, E. Mary. *Jews under Roman Rule, Pompey to Diocletian.* Studies in Judaism in Late Antiquity, vol. 20. Leiden, 1976.

Smith-Rosenberg, Carroll. "The Hysterical Woman," in Esther Katz and Anita Rapone, *Women's Experience in America.* New Brunswick, 1980.

Stagg, Evelyn and Stagg, Frank. *Women in the World of Jesus.* Philadelphia, 1978.

Styger, Paul. *Die römischen Katakomben.* Berlin, 1933.

Styger, P. *Römische martyrbegrüfte.* vol. 1. Berlin, 1935.

Suetonius, *Works.* Edited and translated by J. C. Rolfe. Loeb Classical Library, 1924-30.

Swidler, Leonard. *Biblical Affirmations of Women.* Philadelphia, 1979.

Swidler, Leonard and Swindler, Arlene. *Women Priests: A Catholic Commentary on the Vatican Declaration.* New York, 1977.

Tacitus. *Annales.* Loeb Classical Library. London, 1921.

Tavard, Georges. *Women in the Christian Tradition.* South Bend, 1954.

Tcherikover, Victor. *Hellenistic Civilization and the Jews.* New York, 1959.

Tertullian. *Opera Omnia. Corpus Christianorum Series Latina,* vol. 1. Turnholt, 1954. Translated by R. Arbesman, E. Daly and E. A. Quain in *Disciplinary, Moral and Ascetical Works.* New York, 1959.

Theissen, Gerd. *Soziologie der Jesus bewegung.* Munich, 1977.

Tollinton, R. B. *Clement of Alexandria, A Study in Christian Liberalism.* London, 1914.

Thomas, J. A. C. "Lex julia de adulteriis coercendis." *Etudes offertes à Jean Macqueron,* pp. 635-45. Aix-en-Provence, 1970.

Thurén, Jukka. "Paulus och Gnosticismen." *Svensk Pastoraltidskrift* 30-31 (1982): 569-573.

van Campenhausen, Hans. *Ecclesiastical Authority and Spiritual Power in the Church of the First Three Centuries.* Stanford, 1903.

Volterra, Edoardo. *La conception du mariage d'après les juristes romains.* Padua, 1940.

von Allmen, Daniel. "L'homme et la femme dans les textes pauliniens." *Foi et Vie* 70 (1970). Supp. vol.: 157-181.

von Allmen, J. J. *Maris et femmes d'après saint Paul.* Paris, 1951.

von Rad. *Genesis.* Translated by J. H. Marks. Philadelphia, 1961.

Voöbus, A. *Celibacy, a Requirement for Admission to Baptism in the Early Syrian Church.* Stockholm, 1951.

Warner, Marina. *Alone of All Her Sex: Myth and Cult of the Virgin Mary.* London, 1976.

Welter, Barbara. "The Feminization of American Religion, 1800-60," in Hartman, M. and Banner, L. *Clio's Consciousness Raised.* New York, 1974, pp. 37-157.

Wlosok, A. "Vater und Vatervorstellungen in der römischen Kultur," in Tellenbach, H. *Das Vaterbild im Abendland.* Stuttgart, 1978.

Wolff, Hans J. *Roman Law, A Historical Introduction.* Norman, 1951.
Zscharnack, Leopold. *Der Dienst der Frau in den ersten Jahrhunderten der christlichen Kirche.* Göttingen, 1902.

Index